CW00751607

لشرفة

فيما يجب ى ، وأدعية الأحوال المختلفة

THE GLORIOUS TREASURE

On the knowledge required of a Muslim
and supplications for different occasions

الحبيب عمر بن محمد بن سالم بن حفيظ
بن الشيخ أبي بكر بن سالم

AL-ḤABĪB ʿUMAR BIN MUḤAMMAD BIN SĀLIM
BIN ḤAFĪḌH BIN AL-SHEIKH ABŪBAKR BIN SĀLIM

Translation and Transliteration by
Mohammad Ahmad Mbaye

© 2006CE/1427AH SHEBA PRESS LTD

All rights reserved. No part of this book may be reprinted or utilised in any form or by any electronic, mechanical or other means, now known or hereafter invented, including photocopying and recording, without prior permission from the publishers.

First Edition: 2006CE/Jumada Al-Ula 1427AH

Published by
SHEBA PRESS LTD
Suite 51
Millmead Business Centre
Millmead Road, London N17 9QU
Tel: 020 8801 8001
Fax: 020 885 0060

Translation and Transliteration by
Mohammad Ahmad Mbaye

ISBN 0-9553501-0-7 978-0-9553501-0-8

With special thanks to:

Tahir bin Muḥammad Abunumay, Rahim St. John, Khurom Kiyani, Mohammad bin Abdallah bin Hafidh, Khadija Wolff, Jamil Aslam, Abu Sulayman Riyadh, Madenia Riyadh and Umm Hamid.

CONTENTS

TRANSLITERATION KEY

ء	ʾ	ح	ḥ[2]	س	s	ع	ʿ[9]	م	m
ا	a, ā	خ	kh[3]	ش	sh	غ	gh[10]	ن	n
ب	b	د	d	ص	ṣ[5]	ف	f	ه	h
ت	t	ذ	dh[4]	ض	ḍ[6]	ق	q[11]	و	ū, u, w
ث	th[1]	ر	r	ط	ṭ[7]	ك	k	ي	ī, i, y
ج	j	ز	z	ظ	ḍh[8]	ل	l		

T – Footnotes added by the translator with the consent of the author.

ﷺ – Mentioned after the Prophet Muḥammad's name and translated as "may Allāh bless him and grant him peace."

عليه السلام – Mentioned after the name of a prophet or an envoy of Allāh and translated as "may the peace of Allāh be upon him."

رضي الله عنه – Mentioned after the name of a companion of the Prophet (ﷺ) and translated as "may Allāh be pleased with him."

رضي الله عنها – Mentioned after the name of a female companion of the Prophet (ﷺ) and translated as "may Allāh be pleased with her."

---

1. Pronounced as *th* as in *think.*
2. Strongly breathed *h* produced by a strong expulsion of air from the chest.
3. Guttural *ch* as in the Scottish loch and the German *Aachen.*
4. Pronounced as *th* as in *this.*
5. A heavy *s* the tongue is pressed against the edge of the upper teeth and then withdrawn forcefully.
6. A heavy *d* pronounced far back in the mouth.
7. A heavy *t,* the tongue is pressed against the edge of the upper teeth and then withdrawn forcefully.
8. A heavy *z* pronounced far back in the mouth with the tongue touching the upper teeth.
9. Pronounced by narrowing the passage in the depth of the throat and then forcing breath through it.
10. Pronounced like a French *r.*
11. Guttural *q* sound with a mouth hollowed to produce a full sound.

PREFACE

Al-Dhakhīra al-Musharafa, the work translated here, presents the fundamentals of the *Deen* – obligatory upon every Muslim man and woman – and the appropriate supplications for specific occasions, as documented by the *Sunnah.* The text serves as a manual for both young and old alike; its memorisation is encouraged among children and those new to the religion and it acts as a reminder for the advanced student. It is currently taught at Dar al-Muṣṭafa in Tarīm, and is recommended by al-Ḥabīb 'Umar bin Ḥafiḍh, in his *Maqāṣid Ḥalqāt Al-Ta'līm wa Wasāiluhā,* as the first book to be taught to students of knowledge before the *Bidāyatil-Hidāya* of Imām al-Ghazāli and *Risālat al-Mudhākara* of Imām al-Ḥaddad.

This work, as with all of Ḥabīb 'Umar's works, assists in the practical implementation of the Prophetic *sunna* in everyday life.

ABOUT THE AUTHOR

The *Dāīyah* (Caller to Allāh) al-Ḥabīb 'Umar bin Muḥammad bin Sālim bin Ḥafīḍh al-Ḥusaini, a direct descendent of the Prophet (ﷺ), was born into a scholarly family in the town of Tarīm, Ḥaḍramawt, Yemen on Monday, 4th of Muḥarram, 1383 Hijri (27th May 1963 CE). His early years were spent under the tutelage and guidance of the most eminent *'Ulama* of Ḥaḍramawt at the time, one of whom was his father, the great scholar and *mufti* of Tarīm, the *Dāīyah,* al-Ḥabīb Muḥammad bin Sālim bin Ḥafīḍh. Under their instruction he memorised the Qur'ān and the core texts of the Islamic sciences of *Ḥadith* (Prophetic Tradition), Jurisprudence, *'Aqīdah* (Creed), and all disciplines relating to the Arabic language and to *Sulūk.*

He later moved to the Yemeni town of Bayḍa where he pursued his studies at the *Ribāṭ* of al-Haddar under the renowned Imām al-Ḥabīb Muḥammad bin 'Abdallah al-Haddar, the Shafi'i jurist and scholar al-Ḥabib Zain bin Sumayṭ, and other great *'Ulama.*

In the intervening years he frequently travelled to the land of *al-Ḥaramain* (the two sanctuaries of Makkah and Medina), and received sacred knowledge from the most distinguished *'Ulama* there;

such as the great Imām, al-Ḥabib ʿAbdul-Qādir bin Ahmad al-Saqqaf, al- Ḥabīb Aḥmad Mash-hur bin Ṭaha al-Ḥaddad and al-Ḥabīb Abu-Bakr al-ʿAṭṭas bin ʿAbdullah al-Ḥabshi. He also received *Ijāzas* with various asānīd (chains of transmission) from Sheikh Muḥammad Yāsīn al-Faddani and al-Sayid Muḥammad bin ʿAlawi al-Māliki.

Ḥabīb ʿUmar eventually returned to Tarīm in 1414 H. (1994) and established the Dar al-Muṣṭafa for Islamic Studies, which has become a centre of *tarbiya* (purification and disciplining of the soul), learning and *daʿwah* attracting students and visitors from around the world.

Ḥabīb ʿUmar continues to reside and teach in Tarīm. He has authored a number of books on the teachings and practise of *Islam,* including a *mawlid* celebrating the birth and life of the Prophet Muhammad (ﷺ). His books and audio lectures, widely available throughout the world, continue to gain ground among new audiences with their translation. He has travelled to numerous countries throughout the world in his efforts to revive traditional *Islām.*

AUTHOR'S INTRODUCTION

بسم الله الرحمن الرحيم

الحمد لله رب العالمين وصلى الله وسلم على عبده
المصطفى الامين سيدنا محمد واله وصحبه والتابعين باحسان
الى يوم الدين

وبعد فجزى الله خير الجزاء المحب الموفق المنور
الحريص على نشر الخير محمد بن احمد مباي
على ترجمته لكتيب الذخيرة المشرفه المشتمله
على مبادئ يحتاج اليها المسلم في دينه وادعيه
واذكار جاءت بها السنه يقوى بها الايمان
وتندفع البلايا والمصائب وتدرك الخيرات
والمواهب فبارك الله في خدمته لاخوانه
الناطقين باللغه الانجليزيه من غير الناطقين بالعربيه
بتيسير اخذهم الزاد من المعلومات الاساسيه
والاذكار العظيمه ومن يرد الله به خيرا يفقهه
في الدين (والذاكرين الله كثيرا والذاكرات اعد الله
لهم مغفرة واجرا عظيما)

عمر بن محمد بن سالم بن حفيظ
ابن الشيخ ابي بكر بن سالم

١٤٢٧/٤/٥هـ
٢٠٠٦/٥/٣م

بريطانيا

TRANSLATION OF AUTHOR'S INTRODUCTION

All praise belongs to Allāh alone, the Lord of the World; and may Allāh bless and grant peace to His servant, the Elect (al-Muṣṭafā), the Trusted and Trustworthy (al-Ameen), our master Muḥammad and members of his household and his companions and their adherents; and may that last until the Day of Judgment.

May Allah reward, with the best of rewards Mohammad bin Ahmad Mbaye for his translation of the opuscul *al-Dhakirah al-Musharaffa,* which comprises the essentials a Muslim needs in his religion, plus supplications and invocations as found in the *sunnah.* By them faith is strengthened; trials, tribulations and afflictions are warded off; goodness is achieved, and Allāh's gifts attained. May Allāh bless his service to his English speaking brethren, who are unable to speak Arabic, in making it easy for them to take provision from [these] essential facts and great invocations.

"He whom Allāh wishes immense good for, He grants insight and understanding in the deen" – (Ḥadīth). *And for those males and females who invoke Allāh's name in abundance, Allāh has prepared for them great forgiveness, indeed, and a hugely immense reward* (Qur'ān, 33:35)

'Umar bin Muḥammad bin Sālim Bin Ḥafīḍh
bin al-Sheikh Abu Bakr bin Sālim

1427/4/05

3/05/2006

United Kingdom

بسم الله الرحمن الرحيم

In The Name of Allāh the Most Merciful, the Beneficent

The pillars of Religion are three: *islām, imān* and *iḥsān*[T1].

The pillars of *islām* are five: to testify that there is no god but Allāh and that Muḥammad is His Envoy; to establish the *ṣalāh*[T2]; to give the *zakāh* (alms); to fast in the month of *Ramaḍān*[T3]; and to do *ḥajj* (the pilgrimage) to the House of Allāh (*al-Ka'ba*)[T4] for those who are able to do so.

T1 *Islām* is the submission and acceptance of Allāh's commands, *imān* is faith and *iḥsān* is excellence, or the perfection of faith.

T2 These are the five daily ritual prayers: *Fajr* (dawn), *Ḍhuhur* (noon, immediately after the sun has passed its meridian), *'Aṣr* (late afternoon), *Maghrib* (after sunset) and *'Isha* (Nightfall).

T3 *Ramaḍān* is the ninth month of the Hijri calendar. It originates from the Arabic word *Ramḍ* meaning very hot soil.

T4 To perform pilgrimage to the holy city of Makkah.

The pillars of *imān* are six: to believe in Allāh; His Angels; His revealed Books; His envoys; the Last Day; and predestination – both the good and the evil thereof – whilst recognising that both are from Allāh, Most High.

Iḥsān: is to worship Allāh as though you see Him, and if you can't see Him, to know that He sees you.[1]

---

1 ʿUmar Ibn al-Khaṭṭāb (رضي الله عنه) related that a man appeared before them. He walked up and sat down by the Prophet and asked him about *islām, imān* and *iḥsān*. The Prophet (ﷺ) answered him and then the man departed. The Prophet then said: "ʿUmar, do you know who the questioner was?" I said: "Allāh and His Envoy know best." He said: "It was Gabriel, who came to teach you your religion." (Related by Muslim.)

The full form of this *ḥadith* (tradition) clarifies the pillars of *islām*, *imān* and *iḥsān*. And Ibn ʿUmar relates [from the Prophet (ﷺ)]: "*Islām* has been built on five: testifying that there is no god but Allāh and that Muḥammad is His Envoy; establishing the *ṣalāh*; giving the *zakāh* (alms), making *ḥajj* (the pilgrimage) to the House of Allāh (*al-Kaʿba*) and fasting the month of *Ramaḍān*." (Related by al-Bukhārī and Muslim)

The obligations of *wuḍu* (ablution) are six[2]:

1 – The intention

2 – Washing the face

3 – Washing both hands and arms including the elbows

4 – Wiping part of the head

5 – Washing both feet including the ankles

6 – Doing the actions in order

---

[2] Allāh, Almighty, said in His Book: *O believers, when you go to pray, wash your faces, and wash your forearms to the elbow, wipe your heads, and (wash) your feet to the anklebones.* (Qur'ān, 5:6)

The Prophet (ﷺ) said: "Works are only according to intentions, and a man only receives what he intends." (Related by al-Bukhārī and Muslim on the authority of 'Umar (رضي الله عنه).)

In a *ḥadith* related by Muslim, the Prophet (ﷺ) performed *wuḍu* as it was commanded (in the Qur'ān).

He (ﷺ) also said in the final pilgrimage: "Start with what Allāh has started with." (Related by al-Nasāī with an authentic chain of narration.) Consideration is to be placed on the general scope rather than the specific cause.

The conditions of *wuḍu* are eight:

1 – *Islām*

2 – Discrimination[T5]

3 – Purity from menstrual period or postnatal bleeding

4 – The removal of anything that may prevent water reaching the limbs

5 – That there is nothing on the limbs that may alter the state of water

6 – To know that *wuḍu* is obligatory

7 – An obligatory action should not be confused with a *sunnah*[T6]

8 – The water must be pure[T7] and purifying[T8]

9 – For those with incontinence, or women who have continual vaginal discharge, the entrance of the prayer time and the continuity of one's actions in *wuḍu* are required

---

[T5] *Tamyīz* (discrimination). A child who can eat, drink and clean him/herself after using the lavatory without any assistance is considered to have reached the age of *tamyīz.*

[T6] The Arabic word *sunnah* means that which the Prophet of Allāh (ﷺ) said, or did, or approved of in others, or accepted, or intended to do but did not carry out.

[T7] Free from dirt and impurities.

[T8] To be pure and purifying (*ṭahūr*) the water must be plain, natural water and it must not have been used previously for ablutions.

Du'ā' recited after performing *wuḍu*[3]

أَشْهَدُ أنْ لاَ إلَهَ إلاّ اللهُ وَحْدَهُ لاَشَرِيكَ لَهُ ،
وَأشْهَدُ أنَّ مُحَمَّداً عَبْدُهُ وَرَسُولُه سُبْحَانَكَ اللَّهُمَّ وَبِحَمْدِكَ أشْهَدُ
أنْ لاَ إلَهَ إلاَّ أنْتَ أسْتَغْفِرُكَ وَأتُوبُ إلَيْكَ اللَّهُمَّ اجْعَلْنِي مِنَ التَّوابِينَ
وَاجْعَلْنِي مِنَ الْمُتَطَهِّرِينَ وَاجْعَلْنِي مِن عِبَادِكَ الصَّالِحِينَ.

Ash–hadu an lā ilaha illa -llah waḥdahu lā sharīka lah, wa ash-hadu anna Muḥammdan 'abduhu wa rasūlah. Subḥānaka Allāhumma wa biḥamdika ash-hadu an lā ilaha illā Anta, astaghfiruka wa atūbu ilaika. Allāhumma ij-'alni mina attawābin waj-'alni mina al-mutaṭahirīn waj-'alni min 'ibādika aṣṣāliḥin.

3 'Umar Ibn al-Khaṭṭāb (ﷺ) said that the Prophet (ﷺ) said: "Whoever performs *Wuḍu* and then says 'I testify that there is no god but Allāh, alone, without partner, and I testify that Muḥammad is His servant and His envoy,' will find all eight gates of Paradise open for him. He can enter by whichever he prefers." (Muslim)

I testify that there is no god but Allāh alone, without partner, and I witness that Muḥammad is His servant and His Envoy. I declare Your Glory, *Allāhumma,*[T9] and Your Praise. I witness that there is no god but You, I ask Your forgiveness and turn to You in repentance. *Allāhumma,* make me one of the repentant, one of the purified and one of Your pious servants.

After the *du'ā'* recite *sūrat al-Qadr* (Qur'ān, 97), three times.

T9 Al-Ḥasan al-Baṣri said: "*Allāhumma* is an assemblage of all names through which Allāh is supplicated." Abu-Rajā al-'Uṭāridi said: "The *meem* in *Allāhumma* contains ninety nine names of Allāh." Anndhar bin Shumail said: "Whoever supplicates with *Allāhumma* has asked Allāh by all of His names." Abu Muḥammad al-Baṭlyūsi said: "When one supplicates with *Allāhumma* it is as if saying: 'O Allāh, with all His beauteous names.'"

The pillars of the obligatory prayer (*ṣalāh*) are seventeen:

1. The intention
2. Standing if the person is able
3. The *Allāhu Akbar* of inception
4. Reciting the *Fātiha*[T10]
5. Bowing (*rukūʿ*)
6. Remaining motionless in *rukūʿ*
7. Returning to the standing position (*iʿtidāl*)
8. Remaining motionless in *iʿtidāl*
9. Prostrating (*sujūd*) twice
10. Remaining motionless in *sujūd*
11. Sitting between the prostrations
12. Remaining motionless in the sitting position
13. The last testimony (*tashahud*)
14. Sitting in the final *tashahud*
15. Invoking prayers upon the Prophet Muḥammad (ﷺ) and his family
16. The *salām*[T11]
17. Doing all the above actions in order

T10 The *Fātiḥa* is the opening *sūra* (chapter) of the Holy Qur'ān.

T11 Ending the prayer with *salām*, is to turn the head to the right and say, *as-salamuʿalaikum wa raḥmatu Llah* (peace be upon you and the mercy of Allāh).

The conditions of *ṣalāh* are eight:

1. Purification from both major and minor impurity
2. The removal of any impurity from clothes, the body and the place of prayer
3. Covering the *'awra* [T12]
4. Facing the *qiblah* [T13]
5. The entering of (the prayer) time
6. The knowledge that *ṣalāh* is obligatory
7. An obligatory action should not be confused with a *sunnah*
8. To avoid all that invalidates the *ṣalāh* [T14]

[T12] Areas of the body that must be covered. For men it is from the navel to the knees; for women, it is the entire body except the face and hands.

[T13] Facing the House of God (*al-Ka'ba*), in the Holy city of Makkah.

[T14] Such as talking; laughing; excessive forgetfulness; more than three substantial, consecutive actions; eating; drinking; exposing the *'awrah* if not recovered immediately; the occurrence of impurity if not removed immediately; and preceeding or delaying following the *imām* by two obligatory acts (*arkān fi'liyyah*).

The *du'ā'* for opening the *ṣalāh*[4]

اللهُ اكْبَر كَبيرًا وَالحَمْدُ لله كَثيرا وَسُبْحَانَ الله
بُكْرَةً وَاصيلاً وَجَّهْتُ وَجْهِي لِلَّذي فَطَرَ السَّمَوات وَالأَرْض حَنيفاً
مُسْلِمًا وَمَا أَنَا مِنَ الْمُشْرِكين ، إنَّ صَلاتي وَنُسُكي وَمَحْيَايَ وَمَمَاتي
لله رَبِّ العَالَمين ، لاَشَرِيكَ لَهُ وَبذَلكَ أُمِرْتُ وَأَنَا مِنَ الْمُسْلمين.

Allāhu Akbar kabīrā, wal-ḥamdulilahi kathīrā, wa-subḥān Allāhu bukratan wa aṣīlā. Wajahtu wajhi llilladhi faṭara assamāwāti wal arḍ, hanīfān musliman wamā anā minal-mushrikīn. Inna ṣalāti wa nusukī wa Maḥyāya wa mamāti Lilahi Rabi-l'ālamīn, lā sharīka lahu wabid-halika umirtu wa anā minalmuslimīn.

Allāh is ever Greatest, much praise be to Allāh, Glory to Allāh morning and evening. I turn my face to He Who created the Heavens and Earth, a pure monotheist in submission, and I am not of those who

---

4 Ibn 'Umar (ﷺ) narrated: "While we were praying with the Prophet (ﷺ) a man from among the congregation said: '*Allāhu Akbar kabīra, wal-hamdulilahi kathīra, wa-subhan Allāhu bukratan wa aṣila.*' The Prophet (ﷺ) asked: 'Who said those words?' A man among the people said: 'Me, O Envoy of Allāh.' He replied, 'I was astonished, for by them the doors of Heaven were open.'" Ibn 'Umar [then] said: "I haven't left them since I heard the Envoy of Allāh (ﷺ) say that." (Narrated by Muslim.)

associate (others with Allāh). My prayer, my worship, my life and my
death are for Allāh, Lord of the worlds, Who has no partners. In this
I have been commanded, and I am of the Muslims.

The *du'ā'* of *i'tidāl* (returning to standing after *rukū'*)[5]

رَبَّنَا لَكَ الْحَمْدُ حَمْداً كَثِيراً طَيِّباً مُبَارَكاً فِيهِ مِلْءَ السَّمَوَاتِ
ومِلْءَ الأَرْضِ ومِلْءَ مَا شِئْتَ مِنْ شَيْءٍ بَعْد.

*Rabanā lakalḥamd ḥamdan kathīran ṭayiban mubārakan fihi mil'a-
assamawāt wa mil'a al-arḍ wa mil'a māshi'ta min she'i b'ad.*

O our Lord, all praise is for You, much good and blessed praise, such
as will fill the Heavens and will fill the Earth, and whatever else You
will.

---

[5] Rifa'a bin Rafi (ﷺ) said: "We were praying behind the Prophet (ﷺ). When he
raised his head from bowing, he said: *'Sami'a Allāhu liman ḥamidah.'* A man
behind him said: *'Rabana walaka-lḥamd, ḥamdan kathīran ṭayiban mubārakan
fihi* (O our Lord, praise is for You, many good and blessed praises).' When the
Prophet (ﷺ) completed his prayer he asked: 'Who has said these words?' The
man replied: 'I,' the Prophet (ﷺ) said: 'I saw over thirty angels competing to
write it first.'" (Narrated by Al-Bukhārī.)

It was also related by 'Ali and Ibn Abi'Awfi (ﷺ) that the Prophet (ﷺ) used to
say, when he raised his head from bowing: *"Sami'a Allāhu liman ḥamidah*
(Allāh listens to the one who praises Him)."

The *du'ā'* between the two prostration (*sujūds*) [6]

رَبِّ اغْفِرْ لِي وارْحَمْنِي وَاجْبُرْنِي وَارْفَعْنِي وَارْزُقْنِي وَاهْدِنِي وَعَافِنِي وَاعْفُ عَنِّي.

Rabbi ighfirlī warḥamni wajburni warfa'ni warzuqni wahdini wa'āfini wa'afu 'ani.

O Lord, forgive me, and have mercy upon me, and support me and raise me, and guide me and pardon me, and keep me in good health.

6 Ibn 'Abbas (ﷺ) narrated that when the Prophet (ﷺ) would raise his head from prostration he would say: *"Rabi ighfirli warḥamni wajburni warfani warzuqni wahdini."* (Narrated by al-Bayhaqi in his Sunan.) And in another narration, by Abi Dāud, the *du'a'* continues: "*Wa 'āfini* (and keep me in good health)." (Narrated by Al-Bukhārī.)

The last testimony *(at-tashahud)*:

التَّحياتُ المُبارَكَاتُ الصَّلوَاتُ الطَّيِّبَاتُ لله السَّلامُ عَلَيْكَ أيُّهَا
النَّبي وَرَحْمَةُ الله وَبَرَكَاتُهُ ، السَّلامُ عَلَيْنَا وَعَلَى عِبَادِالله الصَّالحِين
أشْهَدُ أنَّ لاإلَهَ إلاَّ الله ، وَأشْهَدُ أنَّ مُحَمَّداً رَسُول الله

Attaḥi-yātu -l mubārakātu aṣṣalawātu- aṭṭayibātu lilahi. Assalāmu 'alaika ayyuhā-nnabi-yu wa raḥma- tullāhi wa barakātuhu. Assalāmu 'alainā wa 'ala' 'ibādil- lāhi - aṣṣaliḥīn. Ash-hadu anna lā ilāha illa-llāhu, wa ash-hadu anna Muḥammadan rasulullūh.

Blessed Greetings and the Best of Prayers to Allāh. Peace be upon you, O Prophet, and the Mercy of Allāh and His Blessing. Peace be upon us and upon Allāh's righteous servants. I testify that there is no god except Allāh, and that Muḥammad is the Envoy of Allāh.[7]

---

7 Narrated by Muslim on the authority of Ibn 'Abbas (ﷺ) from the Prophet (ﷺ).

The *Ibrāhīmiya* Prayer[8]

اللَّهُمَّ صَلِّ عَلَى مُحَمَّد عَبْدُكَ وَرَسُولِكَ النَّبِي الأُمِي وَعَلَى
آلِ مُحَمَّد وَأزْوَاجِهِ وَذُرِيَتِهِ، كَمَا صَلَيْتَ عَلَى إبْرَاهِيم ، وَعَلَى آلِ
إبْرَاهِيم إنَّكَ حَمِيدٌ مَجِيد وَ بَارِك عَلَى مُحَمَّد عَبْدُكَ وَرَسُولِك
النَّبِي الأُمِي وَعَلَى آلِ مُحَمَّد وَأزْوَاجِهِ وَذُرِيَتِهِ كَمَا بَارَكْتَ عَلَى
إبْرَاهِيم ، وَعَلَى آلِ إبْرَاهِيم فِي العَالَمِينَ إنَّكَ حَمِيدٌ مَجِيد.

Allāhumma ṣalli 'ala Muḥammad 'abduka wa rasulika annabiyul-ummi wa 'ala āli Muḥammad wa azwājihi wa dhuriyatihi. Kamā ṣalaita 'ala Ibrāhīm wa 'ala āli Ibrāhīm innaka Hamīdun Majīd. Wa bārik 'ala Muḥammad 'abduka wa rasūlika annabiyul-ummi wa 'ala āli Muḥammad wa azwājihi wa dhuriyatihi kamā bārakta 'ala Ibrāhīm wa 'ala āli Ibrāhīm fil 'ālamīna innaka Ḥamīdun Majīd.

---

[8] After the recitation of the *tashahud* one should then give prayers and blessings to the Prophet (ﷺ) and his family.
This is the formula of the *ṣalāt al-Ibrāhimiya* that the Prophet (ﷺ) used, as narrated by al-Bukhārī and Muslim (رضي الله عنهما) in their books of *Ṣaḥiḥ*.

Allāhumma, send prayers upon Muḥammad (ﷺ), Your servant and Envoy, the unlettered Prophet; and to the household of Muḥammad (ﷺ), his wives and his offspring, as You sent prayers upon Ibrāhīm and the family of Ibrāhīm; You are truly Most Praiseworthy and Noble. And send blessings upon Muḥammad (ﷺ), Your servant and Envoy, the unlettered Prophet, and to the household of Muḥammad (ﷺ), his wives and his offspring, as You sent blessings upon Ibrāhīm and the family of Ibrāhīm, in all the worlds. You are truly Most Praiseworthy and Noble.

The *du'ā'* after the last *tashahud*[9]

اللَّهُمَّ إِنِّي اعُوذُ بِكَ مِنْ عَذَابِ جَهَنَّم

وَ مِنْ عَذَابِ القَبْر وَمِنْ فِتْنَةِ المَحْيَا وَالمَمَات وَمِنْ شَرِّ فِتْنَةِ المَسِيح

الدَّجَال وَمِنْ المَغْرَمِ وَالمَأَثَم اللَّهُمَّ اغْفِرْ لِي مَاقَدَّمْتُ وَمَا أخَرْت وَمَا

أسْرَرْتُ وَمَا أعْلَنْتُ وَمَا أسْرَفْتُ وَمَا أنْتَ أعْلَمُ بِهِ مِنِّي أنْتَ المُقَدِّمُ

وَأنْتَ المُؤَخِرِ لاَ إلَهَ إلاَّ أنْتَ

---

9 Abu Hurairah (ﷺ) narrated that the Prophet of Allāh (ﷺ) said: "When any of you finish with the last *tashahud* you should ask Allāh for protection from four things: from the punishment of *Jahannam*, from the punishment of the grave, from the tribulations of life and death, and from the evil trials of the *Masiḥ ad-Dajal.*"' (Related by al-Bukhārī and Muslim). And in another narration by Muslim: "When any of you recite the tashahud you should ask Allāh for protection from four things and should say: '*Allāhumma inni a'ūdhu bika min 'adhābi jahannam, wa min 'adhābi-lqabr, wa min fitnatil maḥya wal mamāt, wa min sharri fitnat-almasīḥ ad-dajal.'*"

'Ali (ﷺ) said: "The Envoy of Allāh used to say between the *tashahud* and *taslim*: *'Allāhumma ighfirlī mā qadamtu wa ma akhartu wa ma asrartu wa ma a'lantu wa ma asraftu wa mā anta a'lamu bihi minni anta almuqadimu wa anta almu'akhir, lā ilaha ila Anta.'*"

Allāhumma inni a'ūdhu bika min 'adhābi jahannam, wa min 'adhābi-l-qabr, wa min fitnatil maḥya wal mamāt, wa min sharri fitnat-al-masīḥ ad-Dajāl, wa min al-maghrami walma'athami, Allāhumma ighfirlī mā qadamtu wa mā akhartu wa mā asrartu wa mā a'lantu wa mā asraftu wa mā anta a'lamu bihi minni anta al-Muqadimu wa anta al-Mu'akhir, lā ilāha ila Anta.

Allāhumma, I seek refuge in You from the punishment of the Hell fire, and from the punishment of the grave, and from the tribulations of life and death, and from the evil tribulations of the *Masiḥ ad-Dajal* (False Messiah) and from loss and wrongdoing. *Allāhumma,* forgive me for what I have done and for what I may do, for what I have hidden and for what I have made known, for my excesses and for that which You know better than I. You are the One who advances and You are the One Who inhibits. There is no god but You.

The *du'ā'* of *al-Qunūt*[10]

اللّهُمَّ اهْدِني فِيمَنْ هَدَيْتَ ، وَعَافِني فِيْمَنْ
عَافَيْت، وَتَوَلَني فِيْمَنْ تَوَلَّيْتَ ، وَبَارِكْ لِي فِيْمَا أعْطَيْتَ ، وَقِني شَرَّ
مَاقَضَيْتَ ، فَإِنَّكَ تَقْضِي وَلاَيُقْضَى عَلَيْكَ وَإِنَّه لاَيَذِلُّ مَنْ وَالَيْتَ،
وَلاَ يَعِزُّ مَنْ عَادَيْتَ تَبارَكْتَ رَبَّنَا وَتَعَالَيْتَ فَلَكَ الحَمْدُ عَلَى مَا
قَضَيْتَ نَسْتَغْفِرُكَ وَنَتُوب إلَيْكَ وَصَلى اللهُ عَلَى سَيِّدِنَا مُحَمَّد النَّبي
الأُمي وَ عَلَى أله وَصَحْبِه وَسَلَّم.

---

10 Anas (ﷺ) narrated that the Envoy of Allāh (ﷺ) continued to recite the *Qunūt* in the morning prayers until he left this world. (*Ṣaḥiḥ ḥadīth* narrated by Imām Aḥmad, al-Bazzaz, al-Bayhaqi, al-Ḥākim, al-Daraqṭani, Abdul Razzaq, Ibn Shaibah and others.)

Al-Ḥasan Ibn 'Ali (ﷺ) also narrated: "The Prophet (ﷺ) taught me words to recite while performing the *Witr* prayers: *Allāhumma, ihdina fiman hadait…*(until the end of the *Qunūt*)." (Narrated by al-Nasāi, Abu Dāud, al-Tirmidhi, Ibn Mājjah, al-Bayhaqi with an authentic chain of narration.) And in another authentic narration by Al-Ramahurmuzi: "[He (ﷺ)] taught me words to recite in the *Witr* and *Fajr* prayers." And Moḥammad bin al-Ḥanafiyah, who is the son of 'Ali bin Abi Ṭālib (ﷺ), said: "This is the prayer which my father used to recite in the Dawn prayer in his *Qunūt*."

Allāhumma ihdini fiman hadait, wa 'āfini fiman 'āfait, wa tawalani fiman tawalait, wa bārik li fimā a'ṭait, wa qini sharra mā qaḍait, fa-innaka taqḍī walā yuqḍa 'alaik wa innahu lā yadhilu man wālaita, wala ya'izzu man 'ādaita tabārakta rabbanā wa ta'ālaita, falakal-ḥamdu 'ala ma qaḍaita, nastaghfiruka wa natubu ilaik, waṣala-llāhu 'ala sayyidunā Muḥammad an-nabi al-ummi wa 'ala ālihi wa ṣaḥbihi wa salam.

Allāhumma, guide me among those whom You guide, grant me health among those to whom You have granted health, watch over me among those whom You protect, grant me grace in what You have given me, and protect me from the evil You have ordained. You decree and none decree against You, and none is abased whom You befriend and none is exalted whom You are at enmity with. You are blessed, our Lord, Who are above everything, all praise is Yours for what You decree. I ask Your forgiveness and turn to You in repentance. And may Allāh's prayers be upon *Sayyiduna* Muḥammad, the unlettered prophet, and upon his family and his companions, and [much] peace.

Du'ās to recite after *ṣalāh*

After ending the prayers with *salām*, recite the following:

اسْتَغْفِرُ اللهَ

Astaghfirullah (3 times).

I seek forgiveness from Allāh.

اللَّهُمَّ أَنْتَ السَّلام ، وَمِنْكَ السَّلام وَإِلَيْكَ يَعُود
السَّلام فَحَيِّنَا رَبَّنَا بِالسَّلام وَأَدْخِلْنَا بِرَحْمَتِكَ دَارَكَ دَار السَّلام
تَبَارَكْتَ رَبَّنَا وَتَعَالَيتَ يَاذَا الجَلال وَالإِكْرَم اللَّهُمَّ لاَمَانِع لِمَا
أَعْطَيْتَ ، وَلاَمُعْطِيَ لِمَا مَنَعْتَ وَلا رَادَّ لِمَا قَضَيْتَ وَلايَنْفَعُ ذَا الجَدِّ
مِنْكَ الجَدُّ اللَّهُمَّ أَعِنِّي عَلَى ذِكْرِكَ وَشُكْرِكَ وَحُسْنِ عِبَادَتِكَ

Allāhumma antas-salām wa minkas-salām, wa ilaika ya'ūdu s-salām, faḥayyinā rabbana bis-salām, wa adkhilnā biraḥmatika dārak dāras-salām, tabārakta rabbanā wa ta'ālaita yā dhāl-jalāli wal ikrām. Allāhumma la māni'a limā a'ṭaita, walā mu'ṭiya limā mana'ta, walā rādda limā qaḍaita, walā yanfa'u dhal jadi minka al-jad. Allāhumma a'inni 'ala dhikrika wa shukrika wa ḥusni 'ibādatika.

Allāhumma, You are Peace, and peace emanates from You and to You peace returns; so greet us, Lord, with peace, and admit us, by Your Mercy, into Your House, the Abode of Peace. Blessed are You, my Lord, O Possessor of Majesty and Honour. *Allāhumma*, none can prevent what You have bestowed, none can bestow what You prevent and no wealth can benefit anyone against You. *Allāhumma,* assist me in remembrance of You, gratitude towards You and excellence in Your worship.

Then recite *ayat al-Kursi* (Qur'ān, 2:255).

سُبْحَانَ اللهِ

Subḥān Allāh (33 times).

Glory be to Allāh.

الحَمْدُ لله

Alḥamdulillāh (33 times).

Praise be to Allāh.

اللهُ أَكْبَرْ

Allāhuakbar (33 times).

Allāh is Great.

لاَ إِلَهَ إِلاَّ اللهُ وَحْدَهُ لاَ شَرِيكَ لَه، لَهُ المُلْكُ وَ لَهُ الحَمْد
يُحْيِ وَيُمِيت وَهُوَ عَلَى كُلِّ شَيءٍ قَدير.

Lā ilāha illa-llāh waḥdahu la sharīka lah, lahu-lmulku wa lahulḥamdu yuḥyi wayumīt wa Huwa 'ala kulli shay-in qadīr.

There is no god but Allāh, alone without partners, His is sovereignty and to Him belongs all praise. He gives life and causes death and He has power over all things.

Du'ā' recited when leaving the house[II]

بِسْمِ اللهِ أمَنْتُ بِاللهِ تَوَكَّلْتُ عَلَى اللهِ، وَلَاحَوْلَ وَلَاقُوَّةَ إلاَّ بِاللهِ
الْعَلِي الْعَظِيم

Bismillāh amantu bilah, tawakaltu 'ala-Allāh, walā ḥawla walā quwwata illa billāh al-'aliyi al-'aḍhīm.

In the name of Allāh, I believe in Allāh, I place my trust in Allāh, and there is neither might nor power except with Allāh the Exalted, the Magnificent.

II Anas (ﷺ) said: "The Prophet of Allāh (ﷺ) said: 'Whoever recites, when leaving home: *Bismillāh, tawakaltu 'ala Allāh, walā ḥawla wala quwwata ila billāh al 'aliyu al-'aḍhīm.* It is said to him: 'You have been sufficed, protected, guided,' and Satan will turn away from him and avoid him.'" (Narrated by al-Nasāī and he said it is a good *ḥadīth*). Abu Dāud added: "Satan says to another devil: 'How can you overpower a man who has been guided, sufficed and protected by Allāh?'"

Du'ā' recited when walking to the mosque[12]

اللَّهُمَّ إِنِّي اسْأَلُكَ بِحَقِّ السَّائِلِين عَلَيكَ و
بِحَقِّ الرّاغِبِينَ إِلَيْكَ وَ بِحَقِّ مَمْشَايَ هَذّا إِلَيْكَ فَإِنِّي لَمْ أخْرُجْ أشَراً
وَلاَ بَطَراً وَلا رِيَاءً وَلاَ سُمْعَةً بَلْ خَرَجْتُ إِتِّقَاء سَخَطِكَ وَابْتِغَاء
مَرْضَاتِكَ أسْأَلُكَ أنْ تُعِيذَنِي مِنَ النَّار وَتُدْخِلْنِي الجَنَّةَ وَتَغْفِرْ لِي
ذُنُوبِي فَإِنَّهُ لاَ يَغْفِرُ الذُنُوبَ إلاَّ أنْتَ.

Allāhumma inni as-'aluka biḥaqqi assā-ilīna 'alaika, wa biḥaqqi arrāghibīna ilaika wa-biḥaqqi mamshāya hadha ilaika. Fa-inni lam akhruj asharān, wa lā baṭaran, wa lā riyā-an, walā sum'atan, bal kharajtu it-tiqā'a sakhaṭika wa ibtighā'a marḍātik. As-'aluka an tu'idhani minan-nar watudkhilni al-jannah, wa taghfirli dhunūbi fa-innahu lā yaghfiru-adhunuba illā-anta.

---

12 The Prophet of Allāh (ﷺ) said: "Whoever leaves his house for the prayer and says, *'Allāhumma inni as-aluka biḥaqqi assā-ilīna 'alaika ...'* Allāh will turn towards him and seventy thousands angels will ask forgiveness for him.'" (Narrated, with an authentic chain of narration, by al-Imām Aḥmad, Ibn Khuzaimah, Abu Nu'aim in the *Works of Day and Night,* al-Bayhaqi, al-Ṭabarāni, Ibn al-Sinni and Ibn Mājjah.)

Allāhumma, I ask You by the virtue of those who seek You, and by the virtue of those who desire You, and by the virtue of my walking towards You; I have not set out with insolence or frivolity, nor [have I set out] to show off or to seek fame. Rather, I went out of the fear of Your Wrath and desiring Your Pleasure. I ask You to shield me from the fire and to admit me into Paradise and I ask You to forgive my wrongdoing, verily no one forgives wrongdoing other than You.

Du'ā' recited when entering the mosque[13]

بِسْمِ اللهِ اَللَّهُمَّ صَلِّ عَلَى سَيِّدِنَا مُحَمَّدٍ وَآلِهِ ، اللهم اغْفِرْ لِي ذُنُوبِي وَ افْتَحْ لِي أَبْوابَ رَحْمَتِكَ.

Bismillāh, Allāhumma ṣali'ala sayyiduna Muḥammad wa ālihi, Allāhumma ighfirli dhunūbi waftaḥ li abwāba raḥmatik.

---

13 The Prophet of Allāh (ﷺ) said: "When one of you enters the mosque he should send his salutation to the Prophet of Allāh and his family, then one should say, *'Allāhumma,* open for me the doors of Your mercy,' and when leaving say, *'Allāhumma,* I ask You from Your Virtue.'" (Narated by Abu-Dāud, al-Nasāī, Ibn-Mājjah and others with an authentic chain of narration. It was also narrated by Muslim but he did not include the salutation of the Prophet and his family at the start.) It was also narrated by Ibn-Al-Sinni and he added: "And when someone leaves the mosque he should say, *'Allāhumma!* I seek refuge from Satan.'" (This was also narrated by Ibn-Mājjah, Ibn Khuzaimh and Abu-Ḥātim bin Ḥabbān in their *Ṣaḥiḥs.*)

In the name of Allāh, *Allāhumma,* send blessings and peace upon *Sayyidunā* Muḥammad and his family; *Allāhumma,* forgive all my wrongdoing and open the doors of Your Mercy.

Then step into the mosque with your right foot and make the intention of *i'tikāf*[14] and speak only that which is good.

***Du'ā'* recited when leaving the mosque[15]**

Leave with your left foot, and say:

أعُوذُ بِاللهِ مِنَ الشَّيْطَانِ الرَّجِيمِ وَجُنُودِهِ ، بِسْمِ اللهِ اللَّهُمَّ صَلِّ عَلَى
سَيِّدِنَا مُحَمَّدٍ وَآلِهِ ، اللَّهُمَّ اغْفِرْ لِي ذُنُوبِي وَ افْتَحْ لِي أَبْوَابَ فَضْلِكَ.

A'ūdhu billāhi mina-shaiṭānir-rajīm wa junūdihi, Bismillāh Allāhumma ṣalli 'ala sayyidunā Muḥammad wa ālihi, Allāhumma ighfirli dhunūbi waftaḥli abwāba faḍlik.

I seek refuge with Allāh from Satan and his army. In the name of Allāh, *Allāhumma,* send blessings and prayers to our Master Muḥammad and his family. *Allāhumma,* forgive my wrongdoing and open the doors of Your virtue to me.

---

14 Spiritual retreat in the mosque. It is *Sunna* to do so at any time, but it is highly recommended in the holy month of *Ramaḍān,* particularly in the last ten days of the month.

15 See footnote 13, page 24.

Du'ā's for eating and drinking, and their respective etiquette

When beginning a meal[16]

بِسْمِ اللهِ الرَّحْمنِ الرَّحِيمِ اللَّهُمَّ بَارِكْ لَنَا فِيمَا رَزَقْتَنَا وارْزُقْنَا خَيْرًا مِنْهُ.

(وَزِدْنَا مِنْهُ)

Bismillāh-ir Raḥmān-ir Raḥīm, Allāhumma bārik lanā fīmā razaqtanā warzuqnā khairan minhu.

In the Name of Allāh, the Most Merciful, the Beneficent. *Allāhumma,* bless what You have provided us with and sustain us with food better than this.

---

16 'Ā'isha (ﷺ) relates that the Prophet (ﷺ) said: "When any of you begins to eat he should pronounce the name of Allāh, the Exalted. If he forgets to do it in the beginning, he should say: 'In the name of Allāh, first and last.'" (Narrated by Abu-Dāud and al-Tirmidhi and [they have] said that it is a sound *ḥadīth*). Also 'Abdullāh Ibn 'Amr (ﷺ) said: "The Prophet (ﷺ) would say before eating: '*Allāhumma,* bless what you have provided us with and save us from the punishment of the fire, *Bismillah.*'" (Ibn-Sinni).
Ibn 'Abbas also relates that the Prophet (ﷺ) said: "When Allāh feeds you then say: *Allāhumma,* bless what You have provided us with and feed us with a better food than this. And when drinking milk say: and provide us with more." (Abu Dāud and al-Tirmidhi who said it is a sound *ḥadīth*).

When drinking milk, instead of saying: 'better than this' say: 'and provide us with more' *(wa zidnā minhu)*.

Always eat with your right hand and do not find fault with food.

Upon finishing a meal[17]

Say:

الحَمْدُ لله الَّذي أطْعَمَني هَذَا الطَّعَام وَرَزَقَنيه مِنْ غَيْرِ حَوْلٍ مِنِّي وَلاقُوَّة.

Alḥamdulilāhi-ladhi aṭʿamani hadha aṭ-ṭaʿām warazaqanih min ghairi ḥawlin minni wala quwwah.

All praise is due to Allāh, Who has given me this food and provided it for me without any effort or power on my part.

Always wash your hands before and after the meal.

---

17 Muʿādh ibn Anas relates that the Prophet (ﷺ) said: "He who eats a meal and upon its completion says: 'All praise is due to Allāh, Who has given me this to eat and provided it for me without any effort on my part, or any power;' will have all his preceding wrongdoing forgiven."(Abu-Dāud, Ibn-Mājah and al-Tirmidhi who said that it is a sound *ḥadīth*).

Before drinking

Say:

بِسْمِ اللهِ

Bismillāh

In the name of Allāh

When finished

Say:

الحَمْدُ للهِ الذِي جَعَلَهُ عَذْبًا فُرَاتًا بِرَحْمَتِهِ وَلَمْ يَجْعَلْهُ مِلْحًا أُجَاجًا بِذُنوبِنَا.

Alḥamdulilah aladhi ja'alahu 'adhban furātan biraḥmatihi walam yaj'alhu milhan ujājān bidhunūbinā.

All praise is due to Allāh, Who has made [this water] sweet and wholesome through His mercy, and has not made it salty and bitter on account of our wrongdoing.

Do not breathe into the cup. Drink in three sips.

The etiquette of going to sleep and wakening, and their respective *Du'ās*

Du'ā' recited before sleeping[18]

بِاسْمِكَ رَبِّي وَضَعْتُ جَنْبِي وَ بِاسْمِكَ أَرْفَعُهُ فَاغْفِر لِي ذَنْبِي اللَّهُمَّ إِنْ أَمْسَكْتَ نَفْسِي فَارْحَمْهَا وَإِنْ أَرْسَلْتَها فَاحْفَظْها بِمَا تَحْفَظُ بِهِ عِبَادَكَ الصَّالِحِينَ.

Bismika Rabbi waḍatu janbi wabismika arfa'uhu faghfir li dhanbi, Allāhumma in amsakta nafsi farḥamhā, wa – in arsaltahā faḥfaḍh-ha bimā taḥfaḍhu bihi 'ibādaka aṣṣaliḥin.

---

18 Abi Sa'id al-Khudari (ﷺ) relates that the Prophet (ﷺ) said: "He who says, when laying down to sleep, *Astaghfirullah al-Aḍhim alladhi lā Ilaha illa huwa al-Ḥayyu-l-Qayyumu wa atubu ilaih,* three times, all of his wrongdoing will be forgiven even if they were as abundant as the foam of the sea, the leaves of trees, as numerous as the grains of sand, or the number of days in the world."
Barā' ibn 'Āzib relates that the Prophet (ﷺ) said to him: "When you lie down at night you should wash as you wash for *salah,* then lie down on your right side and say: *'Allāhumma,* I surrender myself to You, turn my face towards You, and entrust my affairs to You. I have entrusted my back to You for protection, in hope and fear. There is no refuge and no escape from You except to You. *Allāhumma,* I have believed in your Book, which You revealed, and Your Envoy, whom you sent.' Then if you die that night you will die in purity and if you awaken in the morning you will encounter more good; and make them the last words you utter. (Bukhārī and Muslim)

In Your name, my Lord, I lay down my side, and in Your name I raise it; forgive my wrongdoing. *Allāhumma,* if You should take my soul, then have mercy on it. If You return it, then protect it, as You guard the righteous of Your servants.

سُبْحَانَ الله

SubḥanAllāh (33 times).

Glory be to Allāh.

الحَمْدُ لله

Alaḥmdulillāh (33 times).

Praise be to Allāh.

الله أكْبَرْ

Allāhuakbar (34 times).

Allāh is Great.

And then say:

أَسْتَغْفِرُ الله العَظِيم الَّذِي لاَ إِلَهَ إِلاَّ هُوَ الحَيُّ القَيُّومُ وَأَتُوبُ إِلَيْهِ.

Astaghfirullāh al-'Aḍhīm alladhi lā ilaha illa huwa al-Ḥayyu-l-Qayyumu wa atūbu ilaih (3 times).

I seek forgiveness from Allāh, the Magnificent, there is no god but He, the Living, Eternal and to Him I repent.

Sleep facing towards Makkah (the *Qiblah*), on your right side, physically pure (with *wuḍu*). Purify your heart from cheating and hate. Make the last words you utter be:

اللَّهُمَّ أَسْلَمْتُ نَفْسِي إِلَيْكَ وَوَجَّهْتُ وَجْهِي
إِلَيْكَ وَفَوَّضْتُ أَمْرِي إِلَيْكَ وَ أَلْجَأْتُ ظَهْرِي إِلَيْكَ رَغْبَةً وَرَهْبَةً
إِلَيْكَ لَا مَلْجَأَ وَلَا مَنْجَى مِنْكَ إِلَّا إِلَيْكَ اللَّهُمَّ آمَنْتُ بِكِتَابِكَ الَّذِي
أَنْزَلْتَ وَنَبِيَّكَ الَّذِي أَرْسَلْتَ.

Allāhumma aslamtu nafsī 'ilaika wa-wajahtu wajhiya 'ilaika wa fawaḍtu amri 'ilaika wa al-jatu ḍhahri 'ilaika raghbatan wa rahbatan 'ilaika la malja wa la manja minka 'ila 'ilaika. Allāhumma āmantu bikitābika aladhi anzalta wa nabiyyaka aladhi arsalta.

Allāhumma, I surrender myself to You, turn my face towards You, and entrust my affairs to You. I have entrusted my back to You for protection in hope and fear. There is no refuge and no escape from You except to You. *Allāhumma,* I have believed in your Book, which You revealed, and Your Prophet, whom You sent.

Then recite *sūrat al-Kāfirūn* (Qur'ān, 109).

Upon awakening[19]

Brush your teeth[T15] (with *miswāk*) and say:

الْحَمْدُ لله الَّذِي أَحْيَانَا بَعْدَ مَا أَمَاتَنَا وَإِلَيْهِ النُّشُور

Alḥamdulillah aladhi aḥyana ba'da mā amātanā wa'ilaihi annushur.

All praise is to Allāh Who has brought us back to life after He had caused us to die and to Him is the return.

---

[19] Ḥudhaifa Ibn al-Yamān (﷦) relates: "When the Prophet (ﷺ) awoke he would supplicate: 'All praise is to Allāh Who has brought us back to life after He had caused us to die and to Him is the return.'" (Bukhārī.)

[T15] It is preferred to brush one's teeth with a *miswāk* taken from the *Arāk* tree. The next most meritorious choice is palm tree, the olive tree, or any other hard object that can perform the task of a toothbrush.

Du'ā' recited when entering the house[20]

When one enters the house say:

اللَّهُمَّ إِنِّي أَسْأَلُكَ خَيرَ الْمُولَجِ وَخَيرَ الْمَخْرَجِ بِسمِ اللهِ وَلَجْنَا
وَبِسْمِ اللهِ خَرَجْنَا وَعَلَى اللهِ رَبِّنَا تَوَكَّلْنَا

Allāhumma inni as-aluka khaira al-mūlaji wa khaira al-makhraji, bismillah walajnā wa bismillah kharajnā wa 'ala-Allāh Rabbana tawakkalnā

Allāhumma, I ask You for the good of entering and the good of exiting. In the name of Allāh we enter, and in the name of Allāh we exit, and in Allāh, our Lord, we trust.

Then recite the [following] verses from the Holy Qur'ān:

﴿ رَّبِّ أَدْخِلْنِى مُدْخَلَ صِدْقٍ وَأَخْرِجْنِى مُخْرَجَ صِدْقٍ وَٱجْعَل لِّى
مِن لَّدُنكَ سُلْطَٰنًا نَّصِيرًا ﴿٨٠﴾ ﴾

(Qur'ān, 17:80)

---

[20] Abi Mālik al-Ash'ari (ﷺ) relates that the Envoy of Allāh (ﷺ) said: "When a man enters his house he should say: *'Allāhumma,* I ask you for the good of entering and the good of exiting. In the name of Allāh we enter, and in the name of Allāh we exit and in Allāh, our Lord, we trust.' Then he should greet his family." (Abu-Dāud). And Abu Hurairah (ﷺ) relates that the Prophet (ﷺ) said: "Within the *sura* (*Al-Baqara*) there is a verse that is the master of verses in the Qur'ān. It is not recited in a house in which Satan is present without him leaving."

Rabbi ad-khilni mudkhala sidqin wa akhrijni mukhraja sidqin waj-'alni min la-dunka sulṭanan naṣīra.

My Lord! Grant me an entry of truth and an exit of truth, and from You, authority to support me.

﴿ رَّبِّ أَنزِلْنِي مُنزَلًا مُّبَارَكًا وَأَنتَ خَيْرُ ٱلْمُنزِلِينَ ٢٩ ﴾

(Qur'ān; 23:29)

Rabbi anzilni munzalan mubārakān wa anta khairu-lmunzilin.

My Lord! Cause me to disembark in a blessed place, for You are the Best to enable [us] to disembark.

Then recite *sūrat al-Ikhlās* (Qur'ān, 112) three times.

﴿ قُلْ هُوَ ٱللَّهُ أَحَدٌ ١ ٱللَّهُ ٱلصَّمَدُ ٢ لَمْ يَلِدْ وَلَمْ يُولَدْ ٣
وَلَمْ يَكُن لَّهُۥ كُفُوًا أَحَدٌۢ ٤ ﴾

Qul huwa' Llahu Aḥad Allāhu- ṣ-Ṣamad lam Yalid, wa lam Yūlad, wa lam yakun'lahu kufuwan aḥad

Say: He, Allāh is One; Allāh, the Eternal, Absolute; He has not begotten, nor been begotten, And equal to Him there is none.

Followed by *ayat al-Kursi* (Qur'ān, 2:255).

Then, offer salutation to whoever is in the house.

Du'ā' recited after the call to prayer *(Adhān)*[21]

اللَّهُمَّ صَلِّ عَلَى سَيِّدِنَا مُحَمَّد وَعَلَى آلِهِ وَصَحْبِهِ وَعَلَى
سَائِرِ الأَنْبِيَاءِ وَالْمُرْسَلِين وَتَابِعِيهِم بِإِحْسَانٍ إِلَى يَوْمِ الدِّين اللَّهُمَّ رَبَّ
هَذِهِ الدَّعْوَةِ التَّامَّةِ والصَّلاةِ القَائِمَةِ آتِ سَيِّدَنَا مُحَمَّداً الوَسِيلَةَ
وَالفَضِيلَةَ وَالشَّرَفَ وَالدَّرَجَةَ العَالِيَةَ الرَّفِيعَة ، وَأَبْعَثْهُ المَقَامَ المَحْمُودَ
الذي وَعَدتَه إِنَّكَ لاَ تُخْلِفُ المِيعَاد.

[21] Jābir bin 'Abdullah (ﷺ) relates that, the Prophet (ﷺ) said: "Whoever says, after hearing the call to prayer (*adhān*): *'Allāhumma,* Lord of this perfect call and of the established prayer, bestow upon Muḥammad *al-wasīlah* and exaltation, and raise him to the praiseworthy station that You have promised him;' it becomes incumbent upon me to intercede for him on the Day of Judgment." (Bukhārī.)

'Abdullah ibn 'Amr (ﷺ) relates that he heard the Prophet say: "When you hear the call to prayer (*adhān*) repeat what the caller (*mu'adhin*) says; then ask Allāh to send blessings upon me, for whoever ask for blessings [to be sent] on me, Allāh sends down blessings on them ten times in return. Then ask Allāh, on my behalf, for *al-wasīlah,* which is a station in Paradise that only one of all the servants of Allāh will be deemed worthy for and I am hoping that I shall be that one. Whoever asks *wasīlah* for me makes it incumbent upon me to intercede for him." (Muslim.)

Allāhumma ṣali 'ala Sayyidunā Muḥammad wa 'ala alihi wa ṣaḥbihi wa-'ala sā'eri al-anbiyā' wal mursalīn wa tābi'ihim bi iḥsānin ila yaumi-ddin. Allāhumma rabba hadhihi adda'wata attama, waṣ-ṣalāti al-qāimāti ati Sayyidunā Muḥammad al-wasīlata walfaḍilata wash-sharafa walddarajata al-'āliyata arrafi'ah, wa-aba'th-hu al-maqāma al-maḥmūdata alladhi wa 'adtahu innaka la tukhlifu al mī'ād.

Allāhumma, send blessings and peace upon *Sayyidunā* Muḥammad, and upon his family and companions, and upon all the prophets and envoys of Allāh and their followers with excellence, to the day of judgement. *Allāhumma*, Lord of this perfect call and of the established Prayer, bestow upon *Sayyidunā* Muḥammad, *al-wasīlah,* and exaltation and honour, and a high and lofty status, and raise him to the praiseworthy station which You have promised him, surely You do not break Your promise.

When rising from a meeting[22]

When you want to rise from a meeting (*majlis*) say:

سُبْحَانَكَ اللَّهُمَّ وَبِحَمْدِكَ ، أَشْهَدُ أَنْ لاَ إِلَهَ إِلاَّ أَنْتَ أَسْتَغْفِرُكَ وَأَتُوبُ إِلَيْك

Subḥānaka Allāhumma wa biḥamdika ash-hadu an lā ilaha illa anta astaghfiruka wa atūbu ilaik.

Glory be to You, *Allāhumma,* praise be to You. I testify that there is no god but You; I ask Your forgiveness and I repent to You.

---

22 Abu Hurairah (ﷺ) relates that the Prophet (ﷺ) said: "If a person sits in company which indulges in vain talk and before standing says: 'Glory be to You, *Allāhumma,* praise be to You. I testify that there is no god but You; I ask for Your forgiveness and I repent to You;' he is forgiven for his participation in that company." (Abu-Dāud, al-Nasāi, Ibn-Ḥabban and al-Tirmidhi who said that it is a sound *ḥadīth*).

Jubair bin Muṭ'im relates: The Prophet (ﷺ) said: "'Glory be to You, *Allāhumma,* praise be to You. I testify that there is no god but You. I ask Your forgiveness and I repent to You.' Whoever says this in a gathering of *dhikr* (remembrance of Allāh) shall have it imprinted on him, and whoever says it in a gathering of *laghu* (vain talk), it will act as forgiveness for him." (Al-Ṭabarāni, al-Nasāi and al-Hākim.)

When entering the lavatory[23]

بِسْمِ الله اللَّهُمَّ إِنِّي أَعُوذُ بِكَ مِنَ الْخُبُثِ وَالْخَبَائِثِ.

Bismillāh. Allāhumma ini a'ūdhu bika mina al-khubuthi walkhabāith.

In the name of Allāh. I seek the protection of Allāh from foul male and female devils.

When leaving the lavatory[24]

الْحَمْدُ لله الَّذِي أَذْهَبَ عَنِّي الأَذَى وَعَافَانِي. غُفْرَانَكَ.

Alḥamdulilah alladhi adh-haba 'ani aladha wa 'āfāni. Ghufrānak.

Praise be to Allāh Who has caused me to remove that which would harm me, and gave me health. I seek Your forgiveness.

---

[23] Anas (🖬) relates that the Prophet (🖬) said, when entering the lavatory: *"Allāhumma,* I seek the protection of Allāh from foul male and female devils."* (Al-Bukhārī and Muslim). In other narration *Bismillāh* (in the name of Allāh) is included.

[24] The Prophet said when coming out of the lavatory: *"Ghufrānak* (I seek Your forgiveness)."* (Abu-Dāud, al-Tirmidhī.) He also said "I seek Your forgiveness. Praise be to Allāh Who has caused me to remove that which would harm me, and gave me health." (al-Nasāī and Ibn-Mājjah.)

When donning a garment[25]

الحَمْدُ لله الَّذِي كَسَانِي هَذَا وَرَزَقَنِيهِ مِنْ غَيْرِ حَوْلٍ مِنِّي وَلاَ قُوَّة

Alḥamdulilah aladhi kasāni hadha wa razaqanihi min ghairi ḥawlin minni wala quwwa.

Praise be to Allāh who has clothed me and provided me with this [garment] without ability or power on my part.

***Du'ā'* for strengthening memory**

اللهُمَّ اجْعلْ نَفْسِي مُطْمَئِنَّة تُؤمِنُ بِلِقَائِك وَتَقْنَع بِعَطَائِك وَتَرْضَى بِقَضَائِك.

Allāhumma ij'al nafsi muṭma'innah, tū'minu bili-qā'ika wataqna'u bi'aṭā-'ika watarḍa biqaḍā-ik.

Allāhumma, make my soul tranquil, believing in [its] meeting You, satisfied with Your provisions and content with Your decree.

To be recited three times in the morning and evening.

---

25 Mu'ādh Ibn Anas (ﷺ) relates that the Prophet (ﷺ) said: "Whoever puts on a new garment and says: 'Praise be to Allāh who has provided me, and clothed me, with this garment without ability or power on my part,' all his wrong-doing – past and future – are forgiven." (Abu Dāud & al-Hākim whith a *ṣaḥiḥ* chain of narration.)

When entering a market.[26]

لاإِلَهَ إِلاَّ اللهُ وَحْدَهُ لاَشَرِيكَ لَه ، لَهُ المُلْكُ وَلَهُ الحَمْدُ ، يُحْيِي وَيُمِيْتُ ، وَهُوَ حَيٌّ لاَيَمُوتُ ، بِيَدِهِ الخَيْر وَهُوَ عَلَى كُلِّ شَيءٍ قَدِير.

Lā ilaha illa Allāh waḥdahu lā sharīka lah, lahu-lmulku walahu-lḥamdu yuḥyi wa yumītu wahuwa ḥayun la yamūt biyadihi al-khair wahuwa 'ala kulli shay'in qadīr.

There is no god but Allāh, alone without partners, Sovereignty is His and to Him belongs all praise. He gives life and He causes death, and He is living and never dies. All good lies in His Hands, and He has power over all things.

---

[26] 'Umar bin al-Khaṭṭab (ﷺ) relates that the Prophet (ﷺ) said: "Whoever enters a market place and says: 'There is no god but Allāh, alone without partners, to Him belongs all dominion and praise. He gives life and He causes death, and He is living and never dies. Good is in His Hand, and He has power over all things,' Allāh will write thousands upon thousands of good deeds in his favour and He will erase thousands upon thousands of his misdeeds, and he will be raised thousands upon thousands of degrees. (Al-Tirmidhi said that it is a good *ḥadīth* and both Ibn-Mājjah and al-Hākim considered it to have a *ṣaḥiḥ* chain of narration.)

Du'ā' for protection from disobedience to Allāh.

اللهُمَّ يَا حَي يَا قَيُوم بِرَحْمَتِك أَسْتَغيث ومِنْ
عَذَابِكَ اسْتَجِير أَصْلِحْ لِي شَأنِي كُلُّه وَلاَ تَكِلْنِي إِلَى نَفْسِي وَلاَ
أَحَد مِنْ خَلْقِكَ طَرْفَة عَيْن.

Allāhumma ya Ḥayyu ya Qayūm biraḥmatika astaghīth, wa min 'adhābika astajīr, iṣliḥ li sha'ni kuluhu, wa lā takilni ila nafsī wala ila aḥad min khalqika ṭarfat 'ain.

Allāhumma! O Living! O Eternal! By Your mercy I call upon You for assistance, and from Your punishment I seek refuge; make good all my affairs and do not entrust me to myself, or any of Your creation, for the blink of an eye. (19 times)

A short biography of the Prophet Muḥammad (ﷺ)

The genealogy of the Prophet Muḥammad (ﷺ)

Muḥammad ibn[27] ʿAbdullāh ibn ʿAbdul Muṭṭalib ibn Hāshim ibn ʿAbdul Manāf ibn Quṣay ibn Ḥakīm ibn Murrat ibn Kaʿab ibn Lū-ay ibn Ghālib ibn Fihr ibn Mālik ibn al-Naḍar ibn Kināna ibn Khuzaimah ibn Mudrika ibn Ilyās ibn Muḍar ibn Nizār ibn Maʿadi ibn ʿAdnān.

The name of the Prophet's (ﷺ) mother

The Prophet Muḥammad 's (ﷺ) mother's name is Āmina bint Wahb ibn ʿAbdul Manāf ibn Zuhra ibn Ḥakīm ibn Murrat ibn Kaʿab ibn Lū-ay ibn Ghālib ibn Fihr ibn Mālik ibn al-Naḍar ibn Kināna ibn Khuzaimah ibn Mudrika ibn Ilyās ibn Muḍar ibn Nizār ibn Maʿadi ibn ʿAdnān.

The Prophet's (ﷺ) wives

The Prophet (ﷺ) married eleven times. Khadīja bint Khuwaylid who is the preferred and most beloved of his wives died before him, as did Zainab. His remaining nine wives died after him.

---

27 The word 'ibn' or 'bin' means 'son of'. For a woman the word 'bint' is used instead, meaning 'daughter of'.

The Prophet's (ﷺ) children

The Prophet Muḥammad (ﷺ) had seven children. Three sons: al-Qāsim, 'Abdullāh and Ibrāhīm; and four daughters: Zainab, Ruqayyah, Um-Kulthūm and Fāṭima az-Zahrā, may Allāh be pleased with them all. All of his children were from his first wife Khadīja except Ibrāhīm, whose mother was Māriya al-Qibṭiya (the Copt).

The Prophet's (ﷺ) battles

He participated in seventy-four battles and twenty-seven expeditions.

His parents and guardians

His father, 'Abdullāh bin 'Abdul Muṭalib, passed away in Madīnah at the age of eighteen whilst he (the Prophet (ﷺ)) was still in his mother's womb. His mother died in al-Abwa[28] when he was only six years old. Guardianship was then transferred to his grandfather 'Abdul Muṭalib who cared for him for a further two years until the time of his death, after which his uncle Abu-Ṭālib cared for him.

Revelation

Allāh sent, and bestowed upon him, the revelation when he passed the age of forty. All preceeding revelations were replaced by his. He emigrated [from Makkah] to Madīnah at the age of fifty-three, where he lived for ten years. He died at the age of sixty-three. May prayers and peace be upon him and his family and may Allāh, on our behalf, reward him with that which is better than what any prophet has been rewarded on behalf of his *Ummah*.

---

[28] A town on the outskirts of Madīnah.

Significant Angels

Angels are beings of light and they are neither male nor female. They do not eat, drink or sleep. The names of the ten most significant angels whose names must be memorised are: Jibrīl (Gabriel), Mika-īl, Isra-fīl, 'Izra-īl, Munkar and Nakīr, Raqīb, 'Atīd, Mālik and Riḍwān.

The revealed Books

It is obligatory to believe in Allāh's revealed Books, the truth inherent in them and that they are Allāh's Word. It is important to know four of these books: the *Tawrat* (Torah), *Injīl* (Evangel), *Zabūr* (Psalms) and the Qur'ān.

Allāh's envoys

Allāh's envoys are many. It is obligatory to believe in them, and in all the prophets. It is also obligatory to believe that they were all trustworthy and veracious. It is required to know the names of [the following] twenty-five envoys:

Ādam, Idrīs (Enoch), Nūḥ (Noah), Hūd, Ṣāleḥ, Ibrāhīm (Abraham), Lūṭ (Lot), Isma'īl (Ishmael); Isḥāq (Isaac); Ya'qūb (Jacob); Ayüb (Job); Yūsuf (Joseph); Shu'ayb; Hārūn (Aaron); Mūsa (Moses); al-Yasa' (Elisha); Dhul Kiefl (Ezekiel); Dāud (David); Sulaimān (Soloman), Ilyās (Elias), Yūnus (Jonah), Zakariyā (Zacharias); Yahya (John), Isa (Jesus) and Muḥammad; Allāh bless them all and give them peace.

How to perform the Funeral Prayer (*Ṣalāt al-Janāzah*)

1. Intend to perform the prayer as a communal obligation and then say *Allāhu Akbar.*

2. Recite *ṣurat al-Fatiha* and again say *Allāhu Akbar.*

3. Invoke blessings on the Prophet (ﷺ) and his family. The best form of blessing on the Prophet is the *Ibrāhīmiya* prayer[T16]. After that say *Allāhu Akbar.*

4. Pray for the deceased, the minimum of which is to say:

اللّٰهُمَّ اغْفِرْ لَهُ وَارْحَمْهُ

Allāhumma ighfir lahu war-ḥamhu

Allāhumma, forgive him and have mercy on him[T17].

5. It is *sunnah* to recite the following verses:

رَبَّنَآ آتِنَا فِي ٱلدُّنْيَا حَسَنَةً وَفِي ٱلآخِرَةِ حَسَنَةً وَقِنَا عَذَابَ ٱلنَّارِ

Rabbanā ātina fi-ddunya ḥasanatan wafil ākhirati ḥasanatan wa qinā 'adhaban-nar. (Qur'ān, 2:201)

T16 See *Ibrahimiya* prayer, page 13.

T17 If the deceased is female then say: اللّٰهُمَّ اغْفِرْ لَهَا وَارْحَمْهَا *Allāhumma ighfir laha warḥamha.*

Our Lord, give us what is good in this world and what is good in the hereafter; and keep us from the torment of the fire.

رَبَّنَا لاَ تُزِغْ قُلُوبَنَا بَعْدَ إِذْ هَدَيْتَنَا وَهَبْ لَنَا مِن لَّدُنْكَ
رَحْمَةً إِنَّكَ أَنْتَ الْوَهَّابُ

Rabbanā lā tuzigh qulūbanā ba'da idh hadaytanā wa hab-lanā min ladunka raḥmatan innaka anta-l-Wahhāb. (Qur'ān, 3:8)

Our Lord, do not cause our hearts to swerve, after You have guided us, and spare us from the torment of the fire

ٱلَّذِينَ يَحْمِلُونَ ٱلْعَرْشَ وَمَنْ حَوْلَهُ يُسَبِّحُونَ
بِحَمْدِ رَبِّهِمْ وَيُؤْمِنُونَ بِهِ وَيَسْتَغْفِرُونَ لِلَّذِينَ آمَنُواْ رَبَّنَا وَسِعْتَ
كُلَّ شَيْءٍ رَّحْمَةً وَعِلْماً فَاغْفِرْ لِلَّذِينَ تَابُواْ وَاتَّبَعُواْ سَبِيلَكَ وَقِهِمْ
عَذَابَ ٱلْجَحِيمِ

Aladhīna yaḥmilūna-l-'arsha wa-man ḥawlahu yussabiḥūna biḥamdi rabbihim wa yuminūna bihi wa yastaghfirūna liladhina āmanū rabbana wasi'ta kula shayin raḥmatan wa 'ilman faghfir lilladhīna tābū wa-ttaba'u sabilaka waqihim 'adhabal-jaḥīm. (Qur'ān, 40:7)

Those who bear the Throne, and those around it, extol the praises of their Lord. They affirm faith in Him, and ask forgiveness for the believers, [saying]: Our Lord! You embrace everything in Your Mercy and Knowledge, so forgive those who repent and follow Your Way, and preserve them from the torment of hell!

رَبَّنَا وَأَدْخِلْهُمْ جَنَّاتِ عَدْنٍ ٱلَّتِي وَعَدتَّهُمْ وَمَن صَلَحَ مِنْ آبَائِهِمْ وَأَزْوَاجِهِمْ وَذُرِّيَّاتِهِمْ إِنَّكَ أَنتَ ٱلْعَزِيزُ ٱلْحَكِيمُ

Rabbana wa-adkhilhum janāti ʿadnin allati wa-ʿadtahum wa-man ṣalaḥa min ābāihim wa-azwājihim wa-dhuriyyatihim innaka anta al-'Azizul-Ḥakīm (Qur'ān, 40:8)

Our Lord, admit them to the Gardens of Paradise, which You have promised them, and [admit therein also] their parents and wives and children who are righteous. For You are the August, the Wise.

وَقِهِمُ ٱلسَّيِّئَاتِ وَمَن تَقِ ٱلسَّيِّئَاتِ يَوْمَئِذٍ فَقَدْ رَحِمْتَهُ وَذَلِكَ هُوَ ٱلْفَوْزُ ٱلْعَظِيمُ

Wa-qihimu assayyiāti waman taqi assayyiāti yauma-idhin faqad raḥimtahu wadhālika huwa-lfawzu-l-ʿaḍhīm. (Qur'ān, 40:9)

And preserve them from all evils, for he whom You preserve from evils on the Day of Arising, to him You have shown great mercy. And that is the immense success.

Then say:

السلام عليكم ورحمة الله وبركاته

Assalāmu 'alaykum waraḥamatullah wabarakātuh.

Peace be upon you and the mercy and blessings of Allāh.[29]

Du'ās recited for the deceased in the *Janāzah* Prayer

Prayers and supplications recited after the third Takbir:

اللهُمَّ اغْفِرْ لَهُ وَارْحَمْهُ، وَعَافِهِ، وَاعْفُ عَنْهُ، وَأَكْرِمْ نُزْلَهُ، وَوَسِّعْ مدْخَلَهُ، وَاغْسِلْهُ بِالمَاءِ وَالبَرَدِ، وَنَقِّهِ مِنَ الخَطَايَا كَمَا يُنَقَّى الثَّوْبُ الأَبْيَضُ مِنَ الدَّنَسِ وَأَبْدِلْهُ دَارًا خَيْرًا مِنْ دَارِهِ، وَأَهْلًا خَيْرًا مِنْ أَهْلِهِ وَزَوْجاً خَيْرًا مِنْ زَوْجِهِ، وَادْخِلْهُ الجَنَّةَ، وَاعِذْهُ مِنَ عَذَابِ القَبْرِ وَفِتْنَتَهُ وَمِنْ عَذَابِ النَّارِ.

Allāhumma, ighfir-lahu warḥamhu wa-'āfihi wa'fu 'anhu wa-akrim nuzulahu wa-wassi'a madkhalahu wagh-silhu bilmā'i walbaradi wanaqqihi minal-khaṭāya kama yunaqqa a-thoubu al-abyaḍ minad-danas, wa abdilhu dāran khairān min dārihi, wa-ahlan khairān min ahlihi, wa-zawjan khairān min zawjihi, wa-adkhilhu-l-jannata, wa-a'idh-hu min 'adhābi-l-qabri wa fitnatahu wamin 'adhābin-nar.

---

[29] The salutation to conclude the prayer.

Allāhumma, forgive him, have mercy upon him, give him peace and absolve him. Receive him honourably and make his grave spacious. Wash him with water, ice and hail. Cleanse him of faults as impurity is cleansed from a white garment. Replace him with an abode better than this abode, with a household better than his household and with a spouse better than his spouse. Cause him to enter Paradise and protect him from the torment of the grave, and its trials, and from the torment of the Hell Fire.

And if the deceased is a child, say:

اللهُمَّ اغْفِر لَه وارْحَمْهُ ، اللهُمَّ اجْعَلْهُ فَرَطًا لأبَوَيْه وَسَلَفًا وَذُخْرًا وَعِظَةً واعْتِبَارًا وَشَفِيعًا ، وَثَقِّل بِهِ مَوَزِينَهُمَا. وَافْرِغ الصَّبْر عَلَى قُلُوبِهِمَا وَلا تَحْرِمَهُما أجْرَه وَلا تَفْتِنَهُمَا بَعْدَه.

Allāhumma, ighfir-lahu wa-rḥamhu, Allāhumma ij'alhu faraṭan li-abawayhi wa-salafan wa-dhukhrān wa-'iḍhatan wa-i'tibāran wa-shafi'ān. Wa-thaqqil bihi mawazinahumā. Wa afrigh aṣṣabr 'ala qulūbihimā wala taḥrimahuma ajrah wala taftinahumā ba'dah.

Allāhumma, forgive him and have mercy upon him. Make him ease the way for his parents; make him a forerunner, a treasure, an admonition, a reflection and an intercessor. Make the scales of their good deeds heavy through him and fill their hearts with patience. Do not deprive them of his reward and do not try them after him.

If one wishes one can add the following *du'ā'*, before the *du'ā'* for the third *takbīr*:[30]

اللهُمَّ اغْفِر لِحَيِّنَا وَمَيِّتِنَا وَشَاهِدِنَا وَغَائِبِنَا وَصَغِيرِنَا وَكَبِيرِنَا وَذَكَرِنَا وأُنْثَانَا, اللهُمَّ مَنْ أَحْيَيْتَهُ مِنَّا فَأَحْيِهِ عَلَى الإِسْلام وَمَنْ تَوَفيتَهُ مِنَّا فَتَوَفَّه عَلَى الإِيْمَان.

Allāhumma, ighfir-liḥayyina wa-mayitina wa-shāhidina wa-ghā-'ibina wa-ṣaghīrina wa-kabīrina wa-dhakarinā wa-unthānā, Allāhumma, man aḥyaytahu minna fa'aḥyihi 'ala-l-Islām wa-man tawafaytahu minna fatawafahu 'alal-imān.

Allāhumma, forgive those of us who are alive and those who are dead, those who are present and absent, those who are young and those who are old, those who are male and those who are female. *Allāhumma,* whomsoever of us You give life to, let us live in Islām and whom soever of us You cause to die, let us die in the state of faith.

---

30 Abu Hurairah (ﷺ) narrates that the Prophet of Allāh (ﷺ) performed the *Janaza* and said: "*Allāhumma,* forgive those of us who are alive and those who are dead, those who are present and absent..." (Abu-Dāud, al-Tirmidhi and al-Bayhaqi. Al-Ḥākim said it is a sound hadith in the condition of al-Bukhari.)

Al-Wird al-Laṭīf

الورد اللطيف

Du'ās for morning and evening

This is a compilation of invaluable and illustrious prophetic invocations by al-Imām Abdallah bin 'Alawi al-Ḥaddad which he named *al-Wird al-Laṭīf.*

بِسْمِ اللَّهِ ٱلرَّحْمَـٰنِ ٱلرَّحِيمِ

1) ﴿ قُلْ هُوَ ٱللَّهُ أَحَدٌ ۝١ ٱللَّهُ ٱلصَّمَدُ ۝٢ لَمْ يَلِدْ وَلَمْ يُولَدْ ۝٣
وَلَمْ يَكُن لَّهُۥ كُفُوًا أَحَدٌۢ ۝٤ ﴾

(3 times)

Bismillāh-ir Raḥmān-ir Raḥīm. Qul huwa Llāhu Aḥad. Allāhu-ṣ-Ṣamad. Lam Yalid, wa lam Yūlad; wa lam yakunlahu kufuwan aḥad. (112)

بِسْمِ اللَّهِ ٱلرَّحْمَـٰنِ ٱلرَّحِيمِ

2) ﴿ قُلْ أَعُوذُ بِرَبِّ ٱلْفَلَقِ ۝١ مِن شَرِّ مَا خَلَقَ ۝٢
وَمِن شَرِّ غَاسِقٍ إِذَا وَقَبَ ۝٣ وَمِن شَرِّ ٱلنَّفَّـٰثَـٰتِ فِى ٱلْعُقَدِ ۝٤
وَمِن شَرِّ حَاسِدٍ إِذَا حَسَدَ ۝٥ ﴾

(3 times)

Bismillāh-ir Raḥmān-ir Raḥīm. Qul aʿūdhu birabbil-falaq min-sharri mā khalaq wa-min-sharri ghāsiqin idhā waqab wa min sharrin naffathāti fil-ʿuqad, wa min sharri ḥāsidin idhā ḥasad. (Qur'ān, 113)

بِسْمِ اللَّهِ ٱلرَّحْمَـٰنِ ٱلرَّحِيمِ

3) ﴿ قُلْ أَعُوذُ بِرَبِّ ٱلنَّاسِ ۝١ مَلِكِ ٱلنَّاسِ ۝٢ إِلَـٰهِ ٱلنَّاسِ ۝٣ مِن شَرِّ ٱلْوَسْوَاسِ ٱلْخَنَّاسِ ۝٤ ٱلَّذِى يُوَسْوِسُ فِى صُدُورِ ٱلنَّاسِ ۝٥ مِنَ ٱلْجِنَّةِ وَٱلنَّاسِ ۝٦ ﴾

(3 times)

Bismillāh-ir Raḥmān-ir Raḥīm. Qul aʿūdhu birabbin-nās malikin-nās ilāhin-nās min-sharril-waswāsil-khan-nās alladhī yuwaswisu fī ṣudūrin-nas, minal-jinnati wan-nās. (Qur'ān, 114)

4) ﴿ رَّبِّ أَعُوذُ بِكَ مِنْ هَمَزَٰتِ ٱلشَّيَـٰطِينِ ۝٩٧ وَأَعُوذُ بِكَ رَبِّ أَن يَحْضُرُونِ ۝٩٨ ﴾

(3 times)

Rabbi aʿūdhu bika min hamazāti'sh-shayāṭin wa aʿūdhu bika rabbi an yahḍurūn. (Qur'ān, 23:97-98)

5) ﴿ أَفَحَسِبْتُمْ أَنَّمَا خَلَقْنَٰكُمْ عَبَثًا وَأَنَّكُمْ إِلَيْنَا لَا تُرْجَعُونَ ١١٥

فَتَعَٰلَى ٱللَّهُ ٱلْمَلِكُ ٱلْحَقُّ ۖ لَآ إِلَٰهَ إِلَّا هُوَ رَبُّ ٱلْعَرْشِ ٱلْكَرِيمِ ١١٦
وَمَن يَدْعُ مَعَ ٱللَّهِ إِلَٰهًا ءَاخَرَ لَا بُرْهَٰنَ لَهُۥ بِهِۦ فَإِنَّمَا حِسَابُهُۥ عِندَ رَبِّهِۦٓ ۚ
إِنَّهُۥ لَا يُفْلِحُ ٱلْكَٰفِرُونَ ١١٧ وَقُل رَّبِّ ٱغْفِرْ وَٱرْحَمْ وَأَنتَ خَيْرُ ٱلرَّٰحِمِينَ ١١٨

Afa-ḥasibtum annamā khalaqnākum ʿabathān wa-annakum ilaynā lā turjaʿūn. Fataʿāla-Llāhu al-Malikul-Ḥaqq lā ilāha illā huwa rabbul-ʿarshil-Karīm. Wa-man yadʿu maʿa Allāhi ilāhan ākhara lā burhāna lahu bihi fa-innamā ḥisābuhu ʿinda rabihi innahu la yufliḥul-kāfirūn. Wa qul-rabbi ighfir war-ḥam wa-anta khairul-Rāḥimīn. (Qur'ān, 23:11-118)

6) ﴿ فَسُبْحَٰنَ ٱللَّهِ حِينَ تُمْسُونَ وَحِينَ تُصْبِحُونَ ١٧

وَلَهُ ٱلْحَمْدُ فِى ٱلسَّمَٰوَٰتِ وَٱلْأَرْضِ وَعَشِيًّا وَحِينَ تُظْهِرُونَ ١٨
يُخْرِجُ ٱلْحَىَّ مِنَ ٱلْمَيِّتِ وَيُخْرِجُ ٱلْمَيِّتَ مِنَ ٱلْحَىِّ وَيُحْىِ ٱلْأَرْضَ بَعْدَ مَوْتِهَا ۚ
وَكَذَٰلِكَ تُخْرَجُونَ ١٩ ﴾

Fa-subḥān Allāhi ḥīna tumsūna waḥīna tuṣbiḥūn, wa-lahu-lḥāmdu fis-samāwāti wal-arḍi wa ʿashiyān waḥīna tuḍh-ḥirūn. Yukhriju al-ḥaya minal-mayyiti wa yukhrijul-mayyita minal-ḥayyi wa yuḥyil-arḍa bʿada mawtihā wa-kadhālika tukhrajūn. (Qur'ān, 30:17-19)

(7 أعُــــوذُ بِاللهِ السَّمِيعِ العَلِيمِ مِنَ الشَّيطَانِ الرَّجِيم

(3 times)

Aʿūdhu billāhi assamīʿ al-ʿAlīmi min-ashshayṭānir-rajīm

(8 ﴿ لَوْ أَنزَلْنَا هَـٰذَا ٱلْقُرْءَانَ عَلَىٰ جَبَلٍ لَّرَأَيْتَهُۥ خَـٰشِعًا مُّتَصَدِّعًا
مِّنْ خَشْيَةِ ٱللَّهِ ۚ وَتِلْكَ ٱلْأَمْثَـٰلُ نَضْرِبُهَا لِلنَّاسِ لَعَلَّهُمْ يَتَفَكَّرُونَ ﴿٢١﴾ هُوَ
ٱللَّهُ ٱلَّذِى لَآ إِلَـٰهَ إِلَّا هُوَ ۖ عَـٰلِمُ ٱلْغَيْبِ وَٱلشَّهَـٰدَةِ ۖ هُوَ ٱلرَّحْمَـٰنُ ٱلرَّحِيمُ ﴿٢٢﴾
هُوَ ٱللَّهُ ٱلَّذِى لَآ إِلَـٰهَ إِلَّا هُوَ ٱلْمَلِكُ ٱلْقُدُّوسُ ٱلسَّلَـٰمُ ٱلْمُؤْمِنُ
ٱلْمُهَيْمِنُ ٱلْعَزِيزُ ٱلْجَبَّارُ ٱلْمُتَكَبِّرُ ۚ سُبْحَـٰنَ ٱللَّهِ عَمَّا يُشْرِكُونَ ﴿٢٣﴾
هُوَ ٱللَّهُ ٱلْخَـٰلِقُ ٱلْبَارِئُ ٱلْمُصَوِّرُ ۖ لَهُ ٱلْأَسْمَآءُ ٱلْحُسْنَىٰ ۚ يُسَبِّحُ لَهُۥ مَا فِى
ٱلسَّمَـٰوَٰتِ وَٱلْأَرْضِ ۖ وَهُوَ ٱلْعَزِيزُ ٱلْحَكِيمُ ﴿٢٤﴾ ﴾

Law anzalnā ḥadhal Qur'āna 'ala jabalin lara-aytahu khāshi'ān mutaṣad-di'ān min khashyati-Llah wa tilkal-amtahālu naḍribuhā linnasi la'Alāhum yatafakkarūn. Huwa Llahu-lladhi lā ilaha illā Huwa 'Ālimul-ghaybi wa-sh-shahādati, Huwar-Raḥmānur-Raḥīm. Huwā Llāhu-lladhi la ilāha illa Huwal-Malikul-Quddusus-Salāmul-Mu'minul-Muhayminul-'Azīzul-Jabbārul Mutakabbir subḥāna-Llāhi'ammā yushrikūn. Huwa-Llāhul-Khāliqu-l-Bāriul-Muṣawwirū, lahul-Asmā'ul-ḥusnā, yusabbiḥu lahu mā fis-samāwāti wal-arḍi, wa Huwal-'Azīzul-ḥakīm.

(9 ﴿ سَلَٰمٌ عَلَىٰ نُوحٍ فِى ٱلْعَٰلَمِينَ ﴿٧٩﴾ إِنَّا كَذَٰلِكَ نَجْزِى
ٱلْمُحْسِنِينَ ﴿٨٠﴾ إِنَّهُۥ مِنْ عِبَادِنَا ٱلْمُؤْمِنِينَ ﴿٨١﴾ ﴾

Salāmun 'ala Nūḥin fil-'ālamīn, innā kadhālika najzil-muḥsinīn, innahu min 'ibādinā'l-mu'minīn.

(10 أعُوذُ بِكَلِمَاتِ اللّهِ التَّامَّاتِ مِن شَرِّ مَا خَلَق

(3 times)

A 'ūdhu bi kalimāti'Llahi tāmmāti min sharri mā khalaq.

(11 بِسمِ اللّهِ الَّذِي لاَ يَضُرُّ مَعَ اسْمِهِ شَيءٌ فِي الأَرْضِ وَلاَ فِي السَّمَاءِ وَ هُوَ السَّمَيعُ العَلِيمِ.

(3 times)

Bismi-Llahi lladhi la yaḍurru maʿa-ismihi shay'un fil-arḍi wa lā fis-samā'i, wa huwas-Samīʿul-ʿAlīm

(12 اللَّهُمَّ إِنِّي أَصبَحْتُ مِنْكَ فِي نِعْمَةٍ وَ عَافِيَةٍ وَ سِتْرٍ، فَأَتْمِمْ نِعْمَتَكَ عَلَيَّ وَ عَافِيَتَكَ وَ سِتْرَكَ فِي الدُّنْيَا وَ الآخِرَةَ

(3 times)

Allāhumma innī aṣbaḥtu minka fi niʿmatin wa ʿafiyatin wa sitr; fa-atmim niʿmataka ʿalayya wa ʿāfiyataka wa sitraka fid-dunyā wal- ākhira.

(13 اللَّهُمَّ إِنِّي أَصبَحْتُ أُشْهِدُكَ ، وَ أُشْهِدُ حَمَلَةَ عَرْشِكَ، وَ مَلائِكَتَكَ، وَجَمِيعَ خَلْقِكَ. أَنَّكَ أَنتَ اللّه لاَ إِلَه إِلاّ أَنتَ وَحْدَكَ لاَ شَرِيكَ لَكَ ، وَأَنَّ سَيِّدُنا مُحَمَّداً عَبْدُكَ وَرَسُولُك.

(3 times)

Allāhumma inni aṣbaḥtu ush-hiduka, wa ush-hidu ḥamamalata ʿarshika, wa malā-ikataka, wa jamiʿa khalqiqa, annaka antaLlahu, lā ilaha ila anta, waḥdaka la sharīka laka, wa anna sayyidunā Muḥammadan ʿabduka wa rasūluk.

14) الحَمْدُ لِلّهِ رَبِّ العَالَمِين حَمْداً يُوَافِي نِعَمَهُ وَيُكَافِيءُ مَزِيدَه

Alḥamdu- liLlahi Rabbil-ʿalamīn, ḥamdān yuwāfi niʿamahu wa yukafi'u mazīdah

15) آمَنْتُ بِاللَهِ العَظِيم، وَ كَفَرْتُ بِا لجُبْتِ وَ الطَّاغُوت،
وَ اسْتَمْسَكْتُ بِالعُرْوَةِ الوُثْقَى لاَ انْفِصَامَ لَهَا وَ اللّهُ سَمِيعٌ عَلِيم

(3 times)

Amantu biLlahil-ʿAḍhīm, wa kafartu bil-jibti waṭ-ṭaghūt, wastamsaktu bil-ʿurwati'l-wuthqa, la'nfiṣāma lahā, waLlāhu Samiʿun, ʿAlīm.

16) رَضِيتُ بِاللَه رَبّاً ، وَ بِالإسْلاَمِ دِيناً ، وَ بِمُحَمَّدٍ صَلّى الله عَلَيهِ
وآلهِ و سَلَّمَ نَبِيَاً وَرَسُولا.

(3 times)

Raḍitu biLlahi Rabban, wa bil-Islāmi dīnan, wa bi-Muḥammadan (ﷺ), *nabiyyan wa rasūla.*

(17 حَسْبِيَ اللهُ لاَ إِلَهَ إِلاَّ هُوَ عَلَيْهِ تَوَكَّلْتُ وَ هُوَ رَبُّ الْعَرْشِ الْعَظِيم.

(3 times)

Ḥasbiy Allahu la ilaha illa Huwa, ʿalayhi tawakkaltu, wa Huwa Rabbul-ʿArshil-ʿAḍhīm

(18 اللَّهُمَّ صَلِّ عَلَى سَيِّدِنَا مُحَمَّدٍ وَآلِهِ وَ صَحْبِهِ وَ سَلِّم.

(10 times)

Allāhumma ṣali ʿala sayyidina Muḥammadin wa ālihi wa ṣaḥbihi wa sallam

(19 اللَّهُمَّ إِنّي أَسْأَلُكَ مِن فُجَاءَةِ الخَير ، وَ أَعُوذُ بِكَ مِن
فُجَاءَةِ الشَّرّ

Allāhumma inni as-'aluka min fuja-āti-l-khayri, wa aʿūdhu bika min fuja-ātish-sharr.

(20 اللَّهُمَّ أنتَ رَبِّي لاَ إِلَهَ إِلاَّ أنتَ خَلَقْتَني
وَ أَنَا عَبْدُكَ ، وَأَنَا عَلَى عَهْدِكَ وَ وَعْدِكَ مَا اسْتَطَعْتُ ، أَعُوذُ بِكَ
مِن شَرِّ مَا صَنَعْتُ ، أَبُوءُ لَكَ بِنَعْمَتِكَ عَلَيَّ وَأَبُوءُ بِذَنْبِي فَاغْفِرْ لِي
فَانَّهُ لاَ يَغْفِرُ الذُّنُوبَ إِلاَّ أنتَ

Allāhumma anta Rabbi, lā ilaha illa anta, khalaqtanī wa ana abduka, wa ana ʿala ʿahdika wa waʿdika māstaṭaʿtu, aʿūdhu bika min sharri mā ṣanaʿtu, abūʾu laka bi-niʿmatika ʿalayya wa abūʾu bi-dhanbi, faghfir li, fa-innahu lā yaghfirū dhunūba illa ant.

(21) اللَّهُمَّ أَنتَ رَبِّي لاَ إِلَهَ إِلاَّ أَنتَ عَلَيْكَ تَوَكَّلْتُ وَأَنتَ رَبُّ العَرْشِ العَظِيمِ

Allāhumma anta Rabbi, la ilaha illa anta, ʿalayka tawakkaltu, wa anta Rabbul-ʿArshil-ʿAḍhīm

(22) مَا شَاءَ اللّه كَانَ ، وَ مَا لَمْ يَشَأْ لَمْ يَكُنْ ، وَ لاَ حَوْلَ وَ لاَ قُوَّةَ إِلاَّ بِاللّه العَلِيِّ العَظِيم

Māshʾā Allāhu kān, wa mā lam yashaʾ lam yakun, wa lā Ḥawla wa lā quwwata illa biLlahil-ʿAliyyil-ʿAḍhīm.

(23) أَعْلَمُ أَنَّ اللّه عَلَى كُلِّ شَيْءٍ قَدِير، وَ أَنَّ اللّه قَدْ أَحَاطَ بِكُلِّ شَيْءٍ عِلْما

Aʿlamu annaAllah ʿala kulli shayʾin qadīr, wa-annaLlaha qad aḥāṭa bi-kulli shayʾin ʿilmā.

(24 اللَّهُمَّ إنِّي أعُوذُ بِكَ مِنْ شَرِّ نَفْسِي، وَ مِن شَرِّ كُلِّ دَابَةٍ أنتَ آخِذٌ بِنَاصِيتَها، إنَّ رَبِّي عَلَى صِراطٍ مُسْتَقِيم

Allāhumma inni a'ūdhu bika min sharri nafsi wa min sharri kulli dābbatin anta akhidhun bi-nāṣiyatiha, inna rabbi 'ala ṣirāṭin mustaqīm.

(25 يَا حَيُّ يَا قَيُّوم ، بِرَحْمَتِكَ أسْتَغِيثُ ، وَمِنْ عَذَابِكَ أسْتَجِيرُ، أصْلِحْ لِي شَأنِي كُلَّهُ ، وَلاَ تَكلْنِي إلى نَفْسِي وَ لاَ إلى أحَدٍ مِنْ خَلْقِكَ طَرْفَةَ عَين

Yā Ḥayyu Yā Qayyūm! Bi-raḥmatika astaghīthu wa min 'adhābika astajīr. Aṣlihli sha'ni kullahu wa la takilni ila nafsi wa lā ila aḥadin min khalqika ṭarfata 'ayn.

(26 اللَّهُمَّ إنِّي أعُوذُ بِكَ مِن الهَمِّ وَ الحَزَن ،
وَ أعُوذُ بِكَ مِن العَجْزِ وَالكَسَل ، وأعُوذُ بِكَ مِن الجُبْنِ والبُخْل ،
وَأعُوذُ بِكَ مِن غَلَبَةِ الدَّينِ وَقَهْرِ الرِّجَال

Allāhumma inni a'ūdhu bika mina l-hammi wal ḥazan, wa a'ūdhu bika minal-'ajzi wal-kasal, wa a'ūdhu bika minal-jubni wal-bukhl, wa a'ūdhu bika min ghalabatid-dayni wa qahrir-rijāl.

(27 اللَّهُمَّ إِنِّي أَسْأَلُكَ العَافِيَةَ فِي الدُّنْيَا وَالآخِرَة اللَّهُمَّ إِنِّي أَسْأَلُكَ العَفْو وَالعَافِيَةَ وَالْمُعَافَاةَ الدَّائِمَةَ فِي دِينِي وَدُنْيَايَ وَ أَهْلِي وَمَالِي

Allāhumma inni as-'aluka al'āfiya fid-dunyā wal ākhira, Allāhumma inni as-'aluka al 'afu wal-'āfiyata wa-l mu'āfāti-d- da'imata fi dinī wa dunyāya wa ahli wa māli.

(28 اللَّهُمَّ اسْتُرْ عَوْرَاتِي ، وَآمِنْ رَوْعَاتِي

Allāhumma-astur 'awrāti wa āmin raw'āti.

(29 اللَّهُمَّ احْفَظْنِي مِن بَيْنِ يَدَيَّ وَمِن خَلْفِي وَعَنْ يَمِينِي وَعَنْ شِمَالِي وَمِنْ فَوْقِي وَأَعُوذُ بِعَظَمَتِكَ أَنْ أُغْتَالَ مِنْ تَحْتِي

Allāhumma iḥfaḍhni min bayni yadayya wa min khalfi, wa 'an yamini wa 'an shimāli wa min fawqi, wa a'ūdhu bi 'aḍhamatika an ughtāla min taḥti

(30 اللَّهُمَّ أَنْتَ خَلَقْتَنِي وَأَنْتَ تَهْدِينِي ، وَأَنْتَ تُطْعِمُنِي، وَأَنْتَ تَسْقِينِي ، وَأَنْتَ تُمِيتُنِي ، وَأَنْتَ تُحْيِينِي وَأَنْتَ عَلَى كُلِّ شَيْءٍ قَدِير

Allāhumma anta khalaqtanī wa anta tahdīni, wa anta tuṭ 'imuni wa anta tasqīni, wa anta tumītuni wa anta tuḥyīni wa anta 'ala kulli shay'in qadīr.

(31 أَصْبَحْنَا عَلَى فِطْرَةِ الإسْلام ، وَعَلَى كَلِمَةِ الإخْلاص، وَعَلى دِينِ نَبِيِّنَا مُحَمَّد صَلَّى اللهُ عَلَيه وَآله وَسَلَّم ، وَعَلَى مِلَّة أَبِينَا إبْرَاهِيمَ حَنِيفاً مُسْلِماً وَمَا كَانَ مِنَ الْمُشْرِكِين

Aṣbaḥna 'ala fiṭratil-Islām, wa 'ala kalimatil-ikhlaṣ, wa 'ala dīni nabiyyina Muḥammadin, ṣalla-Llahu 'alayhi wa alihi wa sallam, wa 'ala millati abīna Ibrāhīma, ḥanīfan, Musliman, wa mā kana mina-l-mushrikīn.

(32 اللّٰهُمَّ بِكَ أَصْبَحْنَا وَبِكَ أَمْسَيْنَا ، وَبِكَ نَحْيَا وَبِكَ نَمُوتُ ، وَعَلَيْكَ نَتَوَكَلُ وَإِلَيْكَ النُّشُور (وَتَقُولُ فِي المَسَاءِ: وَإِلَيْكَ المَصِير)

Allāhumma bika aṣbaḥna, wa bika amsaynā, wa bika naḥya, wa bika namūtu, wa 'alayka nata-wakalu, wa 'ilayka-n-nushūr (maṣir).

(33 أَصْبَحْنَا وَ أَصْبَحَ المُلْكُ لِلّه وَ الحَمْدُ لِلّه رَبِّ العَالَمِين

Aṣbaḥna wa aṣbaḥa-l-mulku liLlahi wal-ḥamdu lil-Llahi Rabbi-l-'ālamīn.

(34 اللّٰهُمَّ إِنِّي أَسْأَلُكَ خَيْرَ هَذَا اليَومِ فَتْحَهُ وَ نَصْرَهُ وَنُورَهُ وَ بَرَكَتَهُ وَ هُدَاه * (وَتَقُولُ فِي المَسَاءِ: هَذِهِ اللَّيلَة)

Allāhumma ʻinni as-'aluka khayra hadha-l-yawmi (hadhihi-l-layla), fatḥahu, wa naṣrahu, wa nūrahu, wa barakatahu, wa hudāh.

(35 اللَّهُمَّ إِنِّي أَسْأَلُكَ خَيْرَ هَذَا اليَومِ ، وَ خَيْرَ مَا فِيه ،
وَ خَيَرَ مَا قَبْلَه ، وَ خَيْرَ مَا بَعْدَه ، وَ أَعُوذُ بِكَ مِنْ شَرِّ هَذَا اليَومِ ،
وَ شَرِّ مَا فِيه ، وَ شَرِّ مَا قَبْلَهُ، وَ شَرِّ مَا بَعْدَ ه
(وَتَقُولُ فِي المَسَاءِ: هَذِهِ اللَّيلَة)

Allāhumma inni as-aluka khayra hadha-l-yawmi (hadhihi-l-layla) wa khayra ma fihi, wa khayra mā qablahu, wa khayra mā baʻdah, wa aʻūdhu bika min sharri hadha-l-yawmmi (hadhihi-l-layla), wa sharri mā fihi, wa sharri mā qablahu wa sharri ma baʻdah.

(36 اللَّهُمَّ مَا أَصْبَحَ بِي مِنْ نِعْمَةٍ أَوْ بِأَحَدٍ مِنْ خَلْقِكَ
فَمِنْكَ وَحْدَكَ لاَ شَرِيكَ لَكَ، فَلَكَ الحَمْدُ وَ لَكَ الشُّكْرُ عَلى ذَلِك
. (وَتَقُولُ فِي المَسَاءِ: اللَّهُمَّ مَا أَمْسَى)

Allāhumma ma aṣbaḥa (amsā) bi min niʻmatin aw bi-aḥadin min khalqika faminka waḥdaka lā sharīka laka, falaka-l-ḥamdu wa laka-shukru ʻala dhalik.

The Translation of *al-Wird al-Latīf*

1) *In The Name of Allāh the Most Merciful, the Beneficent.*
Say: He, Allāh is One. Allāh, the Eternal, Absolute. He has not begotten, nor is He begotten. And equal to Him there is none. (Qur'ān, 112)

2) *In The Name of Allāh the Most Merciful, the Beneficent.*
Say: I seek refuge with the Lord of the Dawn; from the evil of what He has created; from the evil of darkness when it spreads; from the evil of those who blow on knots; and from the evil of the envier when he envies. (Qur'ān, 113)

3) *In The Name of Allāh the Most Merciful, the Beneficent.*
Say: I seek refuge with the Lord of mankind; the King of mankind; the God of mankind; from the evil of the whisperer, the with-drawer; who whispers in the breasts of mankind; from among jinn and men. (Qur'ān, 114)

4) O my Lord! I seek Your protection against the insinuations of the devils and I seek Your protection in their presence. (Qur'ān, 23:97-98)

5) Did you think that We created you in vain, and that you shall not return to Us? Therefore Exalted is Allah, the King, the Truth, there is no god but He, the Lord of the Noble Throne. And whoever calls upon another god with Allāh, of which he has no proof, his reckoning is with his Lord; and the disbelievers will never succeed. And say: My Lord! Forgive and have mercy, for You are the Best of those who show mercy. (Qur'ān, 23:115-118)

6) So glorify Allāh when evening comes upon you and when you rise in the morning. To Him belongs all praise in the heavens and the earth, and in the evenings and in the noon. He brings forth the living from the dead, and [He] brings forth the dead from the living, and He revives the earth after it is dead; and similarly, so you shall be brought forth. (Qur'ān, 30:17-19)

7) I seek refuge in Allāh, the Hearer, the Knower, from the repudiate Satan.

8) Had We sent down this Qur'ān upon a mountain, you would have seen it humbled, rent asunder out of the fear of Allāh. And such examples, We set for people so that they may reflect. He is Allāh; there is no god but He; Who Knows the unseen and the manifest; He is the All-Merciful, the Beneficent. He is Allāh; there is no god but He. He is the Sovereign, the Holy, the Peace, the Faithful, the Guardian, the Eminent, the Compeller, the Proud. Glorified is Allāh above what they associate. He is Allāh, the Creator, the Originator, the Fashioner; to Him belong the Most Beautiful Names. All that is in the heavens and the earth glorifies Him and He is the Eminent, the Wise. (Qur'ān, 59:21-24)

9) Peace be upon Noah among all creation. This is how We reward those who behave with excellence. He was one of Our believing slaves. (Qur'ān, 37:79-81)

10) I seek refuge in the complete words of Allāh from the evil in what He has created. (3 times)

11) In the Name of Allāh, by Whose Name nothing on earth or in heaven can harm. He is the Hearer, the Knower. (3 times)

12) *Allāhumma,* I have risen this morning in Your favour, [with] well-being, and [under Your] protection; so complete Your favour, Your [bestowal of] well-being and Your protection upon me, in this world and the hereafter. (3 times)

13) *Allāhumma,* I have risen this morning bearing witness before You, and bearing witness before the carriers of Your Throne, Your angels, and all of Your creation, that You are Allāh, that there is no god but You, Alone, without partners, and that Muḥammad is Your servant and Your Envoy. (4 times)

14) Praise and thanks be to Allāh, Lord of the Worlds, a praise that is adequate to His favours and equal to His increase. (3 times)

15) I believe in Allāh the Tremendous, and I denounce the idols and false gods, and I hold fast to the firmest handhold, that will never break, and Allāh is [the] Hearer and Knower. (3 times)

16) I am content with Allāh as Lord, with Islām as a religion, and with Muḥammad, may Allāh's blessings and peace of be upon him, as Prophet and Messenger. (3 times)

17) Allāh suffices me; there is no god but He; upon Him I rely; and He is the Tremendous Lord of the Throne. (7 times)

18) *Allāhumma,* send prayers upon our master Muḥammad, his Family and Companions, and give them peace. (10 times)

19) *Allāhumma,* I ask You for immediate good and I seek refuge in You from sudden evil.

20) *Allāhumma,* You are my Lord, there is no god but You, You created me and I am Your servant, and I uphold Your covenant and promise to You, as well as I am able. I seek refuge in You from the evil that I have committed; I acknowledge, to You, Your favours upon me and I acknowledge my wrongdoing, so forgive me, for none forgives wrongdoing except You.

21) *Allāhumma,* You are my Lord, there is no god but You; upon You, I rely, and You are the Lord of the Tremendous Throne.

22) Whatever Allāh wishes, comes to pass, and whatever He wishes not, cannot; there is neither power nor ability save by Allāh, the High, the Tremendous.

23) I know that Allāh has power over everything and that Allāh encompasses everything with His knowledge.

24) *Allāhumma,* I seek refuge with You from the evil of myself and from the evil of every creature You have taken by the forehead; my Lord is on a straight path.

25) O Living! O Sustainer! By Your mercy I appeal for assistance, and from Your punishment I seek protection; make good all my affairs and do not entrust me to myself, or to any of your creation, for the blink of an eye.

26) *Allāhumma,* I seek refuge with You from sorrow and grief, and I seek refuge with You from inability and sloth, and I seek refuge with You from cowardice and miserliness, and I seek refuge with You from the burden of debt and the tyranny of men.

27) *Allāhumma,* I ask of You pardon, well-being and constant safety in my religion, worldly affairs, family and possessions.

28) *Allāhumma,* conceal my faults and assuage my fears.

29) *Allāhumma,* protect me from [the evil that comes] between my hands, and from [the evil] before me, behind me, on my right, on my left, and from above me and I seek refuge in Your Greatness from unexpected harm from below me.

30) *Allāhumma,* You created me and You guide me, and You feed me and You provide me with drink, and You cause me to die and You give me life; and You have power over all things.

31) We enter this morning on the natural disposition of *Islām*; on the Word of Sincerity; on the religion of our Prophet Muḥammad, may Allāh bless him and his family and grant them peace; and on the creed of Ibrāhīm, who was upright, Muslim, and not a polytheist.

32) *Allāhumma,* by You, we have reached this morning and by You, we have reached this evening. By You, we live and by You we die; upon You I place my trust and unto You is the arising.[31]

---

[31] In the evening you say: to You is the final end.(وإلَيْكَ المَصِير)

33) Morning has reached us and unto Allāh belongs all sovereignty, and all praise belongs to Allāh, Lord of the Worlds.[32]

34) *Allāhumma,* I ask You for the good of this day, its openings, victories, illumination, blessings and guidance.[33]

35) *Allāhumma,* I ask You for the good of this day and the good of what is in it, the good of what is before it and the good of what is after it. I seek refuge in You against the evil of this day, the evil of what is in it, the evil of what is before it and the evil of what is after it.[34]

36) *Allāhumma,* whatever favours I, or any of Your creation, receive this morning, will be from You alone; You have no partner, so Yours are the praises and Yours are the thanks for them all.[35]

---

32 In the evening: 'Evening has entered upon us and unto Allāh belongs all sovereignty

33 In the evening: *hadhihil-laylati, fat-ḥaha, wa naṣraha, wa nūraha, wa barakataha, wa hudaha.*

34 In the evening replace 'day' with 'night' (*hadhihi-l-layla* هَذه اللَّيلَة)

35 In the evening replace 'morning' with 'night' (*Allāhumma mā amsa* اللَّهُمَّ مَا أمْسَى)

Commentary on *al-Wird al-Laṭīf*
from

al-Ward al-Qaṭīf fī Takhrīj Aḥādīth al-Wird al-Laṭīf

Commentary of invocations used in the *al-Wird al-Laṭīf*

In the original text al-Ḥabib ʿUmar Bin Ḥafīḍh did not include a commentary on the *Wird al-Laṭīf,* he did, however, refer to the book *al-Ward al-Qaṭif fi Takhrīj Ahādīth al-Wird al-Latīf* of the great *ʿĀlim*, al-Ḥabib Abu-Bakr Bin AbdulRaḥmān bin Shihābuddin, which details the merits of all the invocations contained within the *wird.*

1) *Surat al-Ikhlās*

Abu Hurairah (رضي الله عنه) relates that the Prophet (ﷺ) said: *"Sūrat al-Ikhlās* (Qur'ān, 112) equals one third of the Qur'ān." (Narrated by Muslim.) According to al-Ṭabarāni, Abu-Hurairah (رضي الله عنه) narrates that the Prophet (ﷺ) said: "Whoever recites *sūrat al-Ikhlās* eleven times it is as if he read the Qur'ān four times; and he would be the best among the people of the earth, as long as he fears Allāh."

ʿĀ'isha (رضي الله عنها) narrated that a companion, who led an expedition for the Prophet (ﷺ), would lead the prayer and end the Qur'ānic recitation with *Qul huwa Llahu Aḥad.* When they returned this was mentioned to the Prophet (ﷺ) who said: "Ask him why he does so," which they did. He replied: "It is the attribute of *al-Raḥmān* (The All-Merciful) and I love to recite it." So the Prophet (ﷺ) said: "Tell him that Allāh loves him."

Anas relates that a man said to the Envoy of Allāh: "I love *sūrat al-Ikhlās."* He told him: "Love of it will admit you to Paradise." (al-Tirmidhi)

2 & 3) *Surat al-Falaq & surat al-Nas (al-Ma'uthatayn)*

'Uqbah ibn 'Āmīr relates that once when he and the Prophet (ﷺ) were walking between Juḥaifa and al-Abwā, they were hit by a gust of wind and [were shrouded in] intense darkness. Thereupon the Prophet (ﷺ) began to recite *Qul a'ūdhu birabbil-falaq* and *Qul a'ūdhu birabbin-nās* (*sūras* 113 and 114 respectively). The Prophet (ﷺ) then said: "O 'Uqbah seek protection from Allāh by them, for there is nothing comparable to them when seeking protection." (Narrated by Ibn Dāud)

The *'Alama* Ibn Ḥajjar said, in relation to this hadith, in his commentary on the *Mishkāt:* "There is nothing more effective in removing, and protecting [oneself from] black magic than reading these (*sūras*) on a regular basis, especially after each prescribed prayer, as we have tried [this and found it to be so].

4) *Rabbi a'ūdhu bika min hamazāti...*

It is narrated in a *ḥadīth* that the Prophet (ﷺ) asked for protection against Satan and his followers [with the above formula]. It is also the formula preferred by Imām al-Ḥaddād and is revealed in the Qur'ān in *sūrat al-Muminun* (23:97-98). Imām al-Ghazāli included it among the invocations of *wuḍu* and many *'Ulama* have taken it from him and approved of it. 'Amr ibn Shubaib relates from his father, who in turn related it from his father that: "The Prophet (ﷺ) taught us [the following] words to say when we awoke from our sleep with a start: In the name of Allāh, I seek refuge in the complete words of Allāh from His anger, His punishment and from the evil among His creation; and my Lord, I seek refuge in You from the insinuations of devils and I seek refuge in You, My Lord, in their presence.

5) *Afa-ḥasibtum annamā khalaqnākum...*

Al-Baghawi narrated that Anas said: "'Ali ibn Mas'ud passed by an afflicted man and he recited the verses *Afa-ḥasibtum annamā khalaqnākum 'abathān...* to the end of the *sūrat* (Qur'ān, 23:115-118) and the man was cured; so the Prophet (ﷺ) said: "By the One in Whose Hand lies my soul, if a man with certainty was to read it on a mountain it would perish."

Muḥammad bin Ibrāhīm narrated from his father that the Prophet (ﷺ) sent him on an expedition on which he ordered them to read the above verses in the evenings and mornings. He said they did so and they were protected and victorious.

6) *Fa-subḥān Allāhi ḥīna tumsūna waḥīna tuṣbihūn...*

Abu Dāud narrated in his book of *Sunan* from Ibn 'Abbas (رضي الله عنهما) that the Prophet (ﷺ) said: "Whosoever recites in the morning, *Fa-subḥānaLlahi ḥīna tumsūna waḥīna tuṣbihīn...* until *wa-kadhālika tukhrajūn* (Qur'ān, 30:17-19), will obtain the reward he missed that day; and whosoever recites it in the evening, will obtain the reward he missed that night.

7 & 8) *Aʿūdhu billāhi assamīʿ al-ʿAlīmi min-ashshayṭānir-rajīm*

Maʿqal bin Yasār (ﷺ) narrated that the Prophet (ﷺ) said: "Whosoever recites, *Aʿūdhu billahi assamīʿ al-ʿAlīm minashsyṭānir-rajīm,* three times and recites the last three verses of *sūrat al-Ḥashr* (Qur'ān 59:22-24), Allāh will appoint seventy thousands angels who shall pray for him until sundown, and if he dies that day, he will die a martyr. And whosoever recites these verses at sundown, he shall achieve the same.

9) *Salāmun ʿala Nūḥin fil-ʿālamīn*

Ibn ʿAsākir narrated that Abi Umāmah (ﷺ) said that the Prophet (ﷺ) said: "Whosoever recites in the evening, *Salāmun ʿala Nuḥin fil-ʿālamīn, innā kadhālika najzi'l-muḥsinīn, innahu min ʿibād-inā'l-mu'minīn*, no scorpion will sting him that night.

10) *Aʿūdhu bi kalimāti-Llahit-tāmmāti min sharri mā khalaq*

In *Ṣaḥīḥ* Muslim it is narrated from Abu Hurairah (ﷺ) that the Prophet (ﷺ) said: "Whosoever says at nightfall, *Aʿūdhu bi kalimāti-Llahit-tāmmāti min sharri mā khalaq*, no harm shall affect him.

And in another *ḥadīth* a man came to the Prophet (ﷺ) and said: "What an affliction I received from a scorpion last night!" The Prophet (ﷺ) replied: "If you had said, when night fell, *Aʿūdhu bi kalimāti Llahit-tāmmāti min sharri mā khalaq*, it would not have harmed you."

11) *Bismi-Llahi-lladhi la yaḍurru . . .*

Al-Tirmidhi and AbuDāud narrated that 'Uthmān Ibn 'Affan (🙵) said that the Prophet (🙶) said: "Whosoever says: *BismiLlahi-lladhi la yaḍurru ma'a-ismihi shay'un fil- arḍi wa lā fis- samā'i, wa huwas-Samī'ul-'Alīm,* three times, no harm shall come to them." And in another narration: "No sudden affliction will reach him."

12) *Allāhumma innī aṣbaḥtu minka . . .*

Ibn Assuni narrated that Ibn 'Abbas (🙵) said that the Prophet (🙶) said: "Whosoever says, *Allāhumma innī aṣbaḥtu minka fi ni'matin wa 'afiyatin wa sitr; fa-atmim ni'mataka 'alayya wa 'afiyataka wa sitraka fid-dunyā wal- ākhira,* three times in the morning and evening makes it incumbent upon Allāh to complete His provisions upon him.

13) *Allāhumma inni aṣbaḥtu ush-hiduka . . .*

Abu Dāud narrated that Anas bin Mālik (🙵) said that the Prophet (🙶) said: "When one says, *Allāhumma inni aṣbaḥtu ushhiduka, wa ushhidu ḥamamalata 'arshika…*(until the end of the *du'ā*), Allāh will free a quarter of him from the fire, and if he recites it twice Allāh will free half of him, and if he recites it three times Allāh will free three quarters of him, and if he recites it four times [Allāh will] free him from the fire."

14) *Alḥamdu- liLlahi Rabbil-'ālamīn ḥamdān . . .*

Imām al-Nawawi narrates in his book, *Al-Adhkār,* in the chapter on 'Praise' (*Al-Ḥamd*), that Abi Naṣr al-Tammār, on the authority of Moḥammad ibn al-Naḍhr (رضي الله عنه), said: "Ādam (عليه السلام) said to Allāh: 'O Lord, you have occupied my time with hard work to earn a living, so teach me something that encompasses all praise and all glorification.' So Allāh revealed to him: O Ādam, say three times in the morning and evening, *Alḥamdu- liLlahi Rabbil-'ālamīn, ḥamdān yuwāfi ni'amahu wa yukāfi'u mazīdah.* This encompasses all praise and glorification."

15) *Amantu bi Llahil-'Aḍhīm, wa kafartu bil-jibti...*

Al-Ḥāfiḍh al-Mundhari narrated in *al-Targhīb wa al-Tarhīb* from *Makā'id al-Shaiṭān* of ibn abi al-Dunyā that 'Urwa ibn Zubair would seek protection by reading, three times in the morning and three times at night, *amantu bi'Llahi'l-'Aḍhim, wa kafartu bil-jibtu wat-taghut, wastamsaktu bil-urwatil-wuthqa, lā infiṣāma laha, waLlahu Sami'un 'Alīm.*

16) *Raḍīitu biLlahi Rabban, wa bil-islāmi dīnan...*

Thawbān (رضي الله عنه) narrates that the Prophet (ﷺ) said: "Whoever says, *Raḍitu biLlahi Rabban, wa bil-islāmi dīnan, wa bi-Muḥammadan* (ﷺ), *nabiyyan wa rasūla,* Allāh will suffice him.

Al-Ḥabib Aḥmad bin 'Alawi Jamal al-Layl said that one of the reasons for a good ending (*ḥusna al-khātima*) is diligency in this prayer.

17) ***Ḥasbiya Llahu la ilaha illa Huwa . . .***

Abi Darda (ﷺ) narrates that the Prophet (ﷺ) said: "Whoever says in the morning and evening, *Ḥasbiya Llahu la ilaha illa Huwa, 'alayhi tawakkaltu, wa Huwa Rabbul-'Arshil-'Aḍhīm*: Allāh will suffice all his matters – [both] worldly and in the hereafter.

18) ***Invoking blessings and prayers upon the Prophet* (ﷺ)**

The Prophet (ﷺ) said: "He who invokes blessings and prayers upon me in the morning and evening ten times, my intercession will be incumbent for him." He also said: "Whoever invokes blessing and prayers upon me once, Allāh will bless him ten times."

The *ḥadīths* on the merit of invoking blessings upon the Prophet (ﷺ) are many, and many books have been written on this.

19) ***Allāhumma inni as'aluka min fujā'atil-khayri***

Anas (ﷺ) narrates that the Prophet (ﷺ) used to recite, in the morning and evenings, *Allāhumma inni as'aluka min fujā'atil-khayri, wa A'ūdhu bika min fuja'atish-sharr.*

20) ***Sayyid al-Istighfār* (the Master of Asking Forgiveness)**

In the *Ṣaḥīḥ al-Bukhārī*, Shaddad ibn Aws narrates that the Prophet (ﷺ) said: "The master of *istighfār* (asking forgiveness) is: *Allāhumma anta Rabbi, la ilaha illa anta*...(until the end of the *du'ā'*)," and then he said: "whoever says it with certainty in the morning and dies on that day will enter paradise."

21-24) *Allāhumma anta Rabbi, la ilaha illa ant, ʿalayka . . .*

Ṭāriq ibn Ḥabib said: "A man came to Abi Darda and said, 'O Abi Darda your house is burning!' He replied: 'No it is not. Allāh, Almighty, would never allow that - based on the words I heard from the Envoy of Allāh (ﷺ). Whoever says them at daybreak, no afflication will befall him until night time, and whoever says them at the end of sunset no affliction will befall him until the following morning; *Allāhumma anta Rabbi, la ilaha illa ant, ʿalayka tawakkaltu*...(until the end of the *du'ā*).'" And in another narration: "Nothing that he dislikes will befall him, his family or his possessions, and I have said those words today and they are: *Allāhumma anta Rabbi, la ilaha illa ant, ʿalayka tawakkaltu*... (until the end of the *du'ā*). Then, Abi Darda rose and headed towards his house, and everyone went with him. When they arrived at his house they found that all the surrounding houses had burnt except his house.

25) *Yā Ḥayyu Yā Qayyūm! Bi-raḥmatika astaghithu . . .*

Anas (رضي الله عنه) narrates that when a matter worried the Prophet (ﷺ), he would say: "*Ya Ḥayyu Ya Qayyūm! Bi-raḥmatika astaghithu wa min ʿadhābika astajīr. Aṣlihli sha'ni kullahu wa la takilni ila nafsi wa lā ila aḥadin min khalqika ṭarfata ʿayn.*"

26) *Allahumma inni aʿūdhu bika mina l- hammi wal ḥazan . . .*

Abi-Saʿid al-Khudari narrates that the Envoy of Allāh (ﷺ) once entered the mosque, at a time not appointed for any prescribed prayer, and he saw a man from the *Anṣār*, named Abu-Umāmah, sitting therein. He said to him: "O Abu Umāmah, why do I see you sitting in the mosque at a time not for any prescribed prayer?"

Abu Umāmah replied: "Grief and debts are cleaved unto me, O Envoy of Allāh." The Envoy of Allāh (ﷺ) said: "Shall I teach you some words by which, if you recite them, Allāh will remove your grief and discharge your debts?" He said: "Yes, O Envoy of Allāh." The Envoy of Allāh said: "Say, in the morning and evening: *Allāhumma inni a'ūdhu bika mina l-hammi wal ḥazan, wa a'ūdhu bika minal-'ajzi wal-kasal, wa a'ūdhu bika minal-jubni wal-bukhl, wa a'ūdhu bika min ghalabatid-dayni wa qahrir-rijāl.*" He said: "I did what the Envoy of Allāh asked me to and Allāh removed my grief and discharged my debts."

27-29) *Allāhumma inni as-'aluka al 'āfiya . . .*

Ibn 'Umar(رضي الله عنه) narrates that Prophet (ﷺ) used to recite the following dua in the mornings and evenings: *Allāhumma inni as-'aluka al'āfiya fid-dunyā wal ākhira, Allāhumma inni as-'aluka al 'afu wal-'āfiyata wa-l mu'āfāti-d- da'imata fi dinī wa dunyāya wa ahli wa māli.*

30) *Allāhumma anta khalaqtani wa anta tahd īni . . .*

Samrah bin Jundub (رضي الله عنه) narrates that the Envoy of Allāh (ﷺ) said: "Whoever says in the morning and evening: *Allāhumma anta khalaqtani wa anta tahdīni, wa anta tuṭ 'imuni wa anta tasqīni, wa anta tumītuni wa anta tuḥyīni wa anta 'ala kulli shay'in qadīr,* seven times there is nothing that he askes Allāh that He would not give him."

In his *Wird al-Kabīr* Imām al-Ḥaddad (رضي الله عنه) mentions that this *du'ā* should be recited seven times.

31) *Aṣbaḥna 'ala fiṭratil-islām . . .*

'Abdul-Raḥmān ibn Abri (ﷺ) said that the Envoy of Allāh used to recite, when he rose in the morning: *Aṣbaḥna 'ala fiṭratil-islām, wa 'ala kalimatil-ikhlaṣi, wa 'ala dīni nabiyyina Muḥammadin, ṣalla-Llahu 'alayhi wa alihi wa sallam, wa 'ala millati abīna Ibrāhīma, ḥanīfan, Musliman, wa mā kana mina-l- mushrikīn.*

32) *Allāhumma bika aṣbaḥna*

Abu-Hurairah(ﷺ) narrated that the Prophet (ﷺ) used to say in the morning: "*Allāhumma bika aṣbaḥna, wa bika amsayna, wa bika naḥya, wa bika namūtu, wa ilayka-n-nushūr.*"

33-35) *Aṣbaḥna wa aṣbaḥa-l-mulku li'Llahi . . .*

It was narrated by Abu Dāud Ibn Mālik al-Ash'ari (ﷺ) that the Envoy of Allāh (ﷺ) said: "When you rise in the morning say: *Aṣbaḥna wa aṣbaḥa-l-mulku liLlahi wal-ḥamdu lil-Llahi Rabbi-l-'ālamīn... wa sharri mā fihi, wa sharri mā qablahu wa sharri ma ba'dah,* and in the evening you should say the same."

36) *Allāhumma ma aṣbaḥa bi min ni'matin...*

'Abdullah bin Ghannām (ﷺ) narrated that the Envoy of Allāh (ﷺ) said: "He who says, *Allāhumma ma aṣbaḥa bi min ni'matin aw bi-aḥadin min khalqika faminka waḥdaka lā sharīka laka, falaka-l-ḥamdu wa laka-shukru 'ala dhalik*; has fulfilled his thanks [towards Allāh], for that day; and he who says it in the evening has fulfilled his thanks for that night.

A beneficial *ḥadith*

It was narrated by al-Ṭabarāni in *al-Kabīr* from Abi al-Darda (ﷺ) that the Prophet (ﷺ) said: "Whosoever asks forgiveness for the believing men and women twenty seven times every night, shall surely be of those whose prayer is accepted and through him the people of the world are provided for."[T19]

[T19] In the collection of Prophetic prayers, *al-Madad al-Nabawi*, under the section of 'Prayers after the dawn and evening *Salah*', al-Ḥabib 'Umar Bin Ḥafiḍh recommends that one recites:

اَسْتَغْفِرِ الله الذي لا إلهَ إلاَّ هُوَ الرَّحمن الرحيم الحيُّ القيوم الذي لا يَمُوت وأتوبُ إليه رَبّاً اغفِرلي

(27 Times)

I seek forgiveness from Allāh, the One; there is no god but He, alone, the Most Merciful, the Compassionate, the Living, the Eternal, the Ever-Living, and I repent to Him; O Lord forgive me.

اَسْتَغْفِرِ الله لِلْمُؤمنينَ والمؤمنات

(27 Times)

I ask forgivness from Allāh for all the believing men and believing women.

BIBLIOGRAPHY

Al-Sayyid Aḥmad bin ʿUmar al-Shāṭiri, *Nayl al-Rajā bisharḥ Safinat al-Najā.* Jeddah ʿAlam al-Maʿrifa

Saʿid bin Muḥammad Bā-ʿAshan, *Bushra al-Karīm.* Sanʿāʾ Dar al-Taysīr.

Al-Ḥabib Abu-Bakr Bin ʿAbdul Raḥmān bin Shihābuddin, *al-Ward al-Qaṭīf fi Takhrīj Ahādīth al-Wird al-Laṭīf.* Manuscript.

Shams al-Dīn Muḥammad al-Fāsi, *Sharh Ḥizb al-Nawawi.* Dar Imām Muslim.

Al al-Ḥabib ʿUmar Bin Ḥafiḍh, *Khulāṣat al-Madad al-Nabawī fi Awarād āl-Bāʿ Alawī.* Tarīm Hadhramout Dār al-Faqīh

Zaki al-Deen ʿAbdul-ʿAḍhim ibn Abdul-Qawi Al-Mundhari *al-Targhib wa al-Tarhimb.* Beirut, Dar al-Jeel

Aḥmad bin Muḥammad bin ʿAli al-Muqri *Al-Miṣbaḥ al-Munīr.* Beirut
al-Maktabah al-ʿAlamiyah

Abu al-Qāsim Maḥmüd bin ʿUmar Al-Zamakhshari *Asās al-Balāgha*

Al-Ḥabib ʿUmar bin Muḥammad bin Sālim bin Ḥafiḍh, *Maqāṣid Ḥalaqātb al-Taʿlīm wa Wasāiluhā.* Bidha Yemen Maktaba al-Muhājir

The Majestic Qur'ān, The Nawawi Foundation Chicago, The Ibn Khaldun Foundation London.

A. Yousef 'Ali, The Holy Qur'ān Translation and Commentary. Beirut Dar al- Qur'ān.

Imām 'Abdallah bin 'Alawi al-Ḥaddad, The Prophetic Invocations. Translated by Mostafa al-Badawi. The Starlatch Press, Burr Ridge USA.

Hans Wehr, A Dictionary of Modern Written Arabic.London Macdonald & Evans Ltd, Beirut Libraire Du Liban.

Muḥammad Zafrulla Khan. Gardens of The Righteous, Olive Branch Press Brooklyn New York Olive Branch Press Brooklyn New York.